LIBRARY STORY HOUR
from A to Z

❤❤❤❤❤

LIBRARY STORY HOUR
from A to Z

♥♥♥♥♥

Ready-to-Use Alphabet Activities for Young Learners

ELLEN K. HASBROUCK

THE CENTER FOR APPLIED RESEARCH IN EDUCATION
West Nyack, New York 10994

Library of Congress Cataloging-in-Publication Data

Hasbrouck, Ellen K.
   Library story hour from A to Z / Ellen K. Hasbrouck.
     p. cm.
   ISBN 0-87628-895-6
   1. English language—Alphabet—Study and teaching (Primary)—Activity programs—United States.   2. Children's libraries—Activity programs—United States.   3. Storytelling—United States.   I. Title.
LB1525.65.H37 1997
421'.1—dc21

                                                       97-39859
                                                           CIP

Printed in the United States of America

10 9 8 7 6 5 4 3 2 1

ISBN 0-87628-895-6

THE CENTER FOR APPLIED RESEARCH IN EDUCATION
West Nyack, NY 10994
A Simon & Schuster Company

On the World Wide Web at http://www.phdirect.com

Prentice Hall International (UK) Limited, *London*
Prentice Hall of Australia Pty. Limited, *Sydney*
Prentice Hall Canada, Inc., *Toronto*
Prentice Hall Hispanoamericana, S.A., *Mexico*
Prentice Hall of India Private Limited, *New Delhi*
Prentice Hall of Japan, Inc., *Tokyo*
Simon & Schuster Asia Pte. Ltd., *Singapore*
Editora Prentice Hall do Brasil, Ltda., *Rio de Janeiro*

About the Author

Ellen Hasbrouck is the school librarian for the Bethlehem-Center Elementary School in Fredericktown, Pennsylvania. Prior to that, she was a public librarian and the author of numerous articles in professional publications. A graduate of Thiel College, she earned her elementary certification at California University of Pennsylvania, her library certification at Slippery Rock University of Pennsylvania, and her MLS at the University of Pittsburgh.

Contents

Undersea World **201**

Vacation **217**

Weather **231**

"X-tra" Ideas **241**

Alligators

Getting Ready to Teach the Letter A

You might want to set the scene for this unit by creating a "swamp" in the story area. Place blue or green bed sheets or tablecloths on the floor. Lengths of brown felt, measuring 18 inches by 72 inches, can serve as logs. Children can sit on the logs for the duration of the story. An audio cassette of Everglades sounds is available from: Music Company, 7692 Zionsville Road, Indianapolis, IN 46268.

Objectives for Alligators:

Each child will be able to:

1. Match the letter "A" with the word "alligator" and vice versa.
2. Summarize the read-aloud story in chronological order.
3. Describe an alligator's habitat, its eating habits, and its physical characteristics.

Introductory Activity: Alligator Roll

Materials:

- one roll of paper towels (or any roll of paper at least twelve feet long and nine inches wide)
- scissors
- wide, felt-tipped marker

Preparation:

Tear off a twelve-foot length of paper towels (about 16 towels). Using the sketch below, draw an alligator on the towel and cut it out. Use a felt-tipped marker to write an alligator fact, listed below, on every other towel rectangle, ending with the last fact on the alligator snout. Roll up the towel, starting with the head and ending with the tail.

Procedure:

Choose several students to help support the alligator as you unroll it. Standing in front of the room, slowly unroll the alligator, reading each of the alligator facts as you go:

- I am going to tell you about a very interesting animal. This animal can live as long as 40 years.
- This animal first appeared more than 35 million years ago. It has about 34 to 40 sharp teeth.

- This animal eats food as small as crayfish and water beetles and as large as pigs, mules, and deer.
- It lays between 20 to 60 eggs at a time.
- No other reptile cares for its young as well as this animal.
- A thin skin covers this animal's eyes so it can see underwater.
- But the most interesting thing about this animal is that it can grow up to twelve feet long. Can you guess what animal this is?

Recommended Books

Alligator **by Evelyn Shaw, illustrated by Frances Zweifel** (New York: Harper & Row, 1972); two-color illustrations; Interest Level: K-3; Reading Level: 2.1.

Despite interference from a hunter, a mother alligator prepares and guards her nest as her eggs hatch.

Alligator Shoes **by Arthur Dorros** (New York: Dutton Children's Books, 1982); two-color illustrations; Interest Level: K-3; Reading Level: 1.6.

An alligator named Alvin tries on many pairs of shoes until he decides that he likes his alligator feet best of all.

The Alligator Under the Bed **by Joan Lowery Nixon, illustrated by Jan Hughes** (New York: G.P. Putnam's Sons, 1974); two-color illustrations; Interest Level: K-3.

Loveable Uncle Harry humorously helps his niece get rid of the alligator under her bed.

Alligators All Around: An Alphabet **by Maurice Sendak** (New York: Harper & Row, 1962); two-color illustrations; Interest Level: K-3; Reading Level: 2.6.

Zany alligators demonstrate the letters of the alphabet with their antics.

Clive Eats Alligators **by Alison Lester** (Boston: Houghton Mifflin, 1986); full-color illustrations; Interest Level: PreK-3; Reading Level: 3.0.

Presents the everyday routine of seven children, each of whom has a special idiosyncrasy.

Gator Pie **by Louise Mathews, illustrated by Jeni Bassett** (New York: Dodd, Mead & Co., 1979); full-color illustrations; Interest Level: K-3; Reading Level: 3.1.

Two young alligators think they will have to share their pie with 98 other alligators.

Mama Don't Allow: Starring Miles and the Swamp Band **by Thatcher Hurd** (New York: Harper & Row, 1984); full-color illustrations; Interest Level: K-3; Reading Level: 2.8.

The Swamp Band plays at the wild Alligator Ball and tricks the alligators from eating the band members at the conclusion of the ball by playing soft music and lulling the alligators to sleep.

Norman Fools the Tooth Fairy **by Carol Carrick, illustrated by Lisa McCue** (New York: Scholastic, 1992); full-color illustrations; Interest Level: K-3; Reading Level: 3.9.

When Norman fails to lose his tooth, he tries to deceive the tooth fairy by putting a false tooth under his pillow.

Swampy Alligator **by Jack Gantos, illustrated by Nicole Rubel** (New York: Windmill/Wanderer, 1980); three-color illustrations; Interest Level: K-3; Reading Level: 1.7.

Swampy the Alligator can't understand why his friends are repelled by his swampy odor, but they clean him up just in time for his birthday party.

***Use Your Head, Dear* by Aliki** (New York: Greenwillow, 1983); black/white/green illustrations; Interest Level: K-3; Reading Level: 2.6.

A pair of alligator parents devise a plan to help their absent-minded son.

***Zack's Alligator Goes to School* by Shirley Mozelle, illustrated by James Watts** (New York: HarperCollins, 1994); full-color illustrations; Interest Level: K-3; Reading Level: 1.7.

Zack takes an alligator key chain to school which grows into a friendly alligator and turns the classroom upside-down with his antics.

Nonfiction Resources

***All About Alligators* written and illustrated by Jim Arnosky** (New York: Scholastic, 1994); full-color illustrations; Interest Level: K-3; Reading Level: not listed.

Text and illustrations describe the habits, habitats, and attributes of alligators.

***Amazing Crocodiles & Reptiles* by Mary Ling, photographed by Jerry Young** (New York: Alfred A. Knopf, 1991); full-color photographs and illustrations; Interest Level: K-3; Reading Level: 5.3.

Presents photos and text about the life cycle and physical characteristics of various reptiles, including alligators.

***Crocodiles and Alligators* by Susan Harris, illustrated by Tim Bramfitt** (New York: Franklin Watts, 1985); full-color illustrations; Interest Level: K-3; Reading Level: 4.7.

Describes physical characteristics, habits, and life cycle of crocodiles and alligators.

***Never Kiss an Alligator* written and photographed by Colleen Stanley Bare** (New York: Cobblehill Books (Puffin), 1989); full-color photographs; Interest Level: K-3; Reading Level: 4.8.

Contains information about the habits, habitat, and characteristics of alligators.

***What Is a Reptile?* by Susan Kuchalla, illustrated by Paul Harvey** (Mahwah, NJ: Troll Associates, 1982); full-color illustrations; Interest Level: K-3; Reading Level: 2.7.

Presents a variety of reptiles and explains the animals' major characteristics.

Recipe: Alligator Cookies

1/2 cup smooth peanut butter

1/2 cup honey

1 cup powdered milk

1 2.25-ounce container cinnamon decors

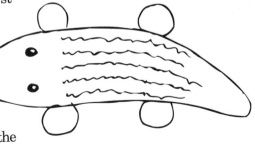

(This recipe makes about 9 alligators.) Mix the first three ingredients, kneading the dough until it is consistently smooth. Pinch off dough to create a 1-1/2-inch ball and four 1/2-inch balls. Roll the large ball into a 3-inch log, tapering one end of the log to resemble an alligator tail. Place two cinnamon candies on the log to represent alligator eyes. Place the 1/2-inch balls on the sides of the log to represent alligator legs. Use the tines of a fork to create alligator scales.

Music Activity: "Alligator Song"

Two students stand facing each other, join hands, and raise their hands above their heads to create "alligator jaws." The other children form a continuous line and, one-by-one, walk under the alligator jaws while, at the same time, singing the first verse of the song. When the children sing "froggies," the last word in the first verse, the two children forming the alligator jaws lower their arms to surround the child who is between them. During the second verse, the two children keep their arms lowered, swinging them gently to and fro, while the rest of the class continues to sing the second verse. At the conclusion of the second verse, choose two other children to form the alligator jaws and continue as before.

ALLIGATOR SONG (Sung to the tune "London Bridge.")

Verse 2:   Alligators will gobble frogs up,
             Gobble frogs up, Gobble frogs up.
             Alligators will gobble frogs up,
             Poor, poor froggies

Art Activity: Alligator Neck Pouch

Materials:
- photocopies of alligator purse pattern
- yarn
- safety scissors
- crayons
- tape
- paper punch

Preparation:
Photocopy alligator purse pattern. Use a paper punch to make two holes on the top corners of the pouch pattern. Cut yarn into 18-inch lengths.

Procedure:
Distribute an unfinished pouch and a length of yarn to each child. Have students color the pouch. Fold along the fold lines and tape side A to side B and side C to side D to create a pocket. Thread the string through the holes and tie at the top to create a pouch the student can wear around his or her neck.

Side A

Side B

Tape this edge to Side A.

Tape this edge to Side B.

Alligator Purse Pattern

Name _____ Date _____

Classroom Teacher _____

Alligators Research Project: Alligators, according to some sources, are endangered species. Look up "endangered species" in a world almanac or other reference source. Write the names of five other endangered species on the lines below. Include the title of the book where you found your information.

1. _____

_____

2. _____

_____

3. _____

_____

4. _____

_____

5. _____

_____

Alligator Dancing the Macarena

Bubbles

Getting Ready to Teach the Letter B

Turn this unit into a bubble party! Encourage the students to wear a shower cap and bathrobe over their regular clothes. You might also want to distribute sugarless bubble gum to the students before the activities begin. Send the following letter home a week before you begin the bubbles activities.

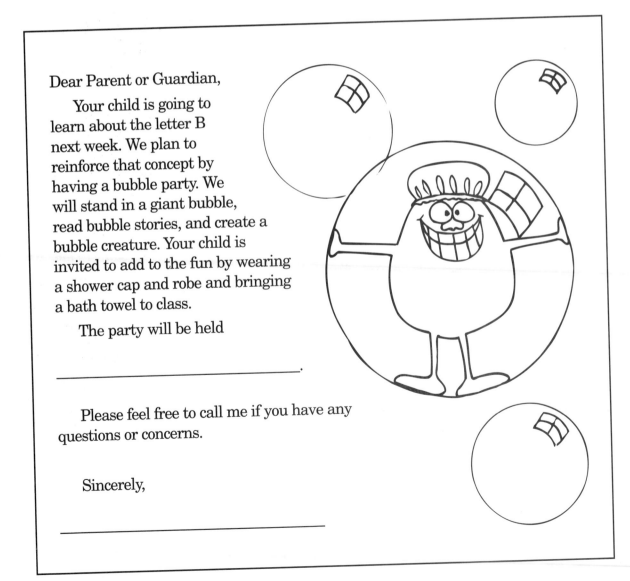

Dear Parent or Guardian,

Your child is going to learn about the letter B next week. We plan to reinforce that concept by having a bubble party. We will stand in a giant bubble, read bubble stories, and create a bubble creature. Your child is invited to add to the fun by wearing a shower cap and robe and bringing a bath towel to class.

The party will be held

_____.

Please feel free to call me if you have any questions or concerns.

Sincerely,

_____

Objectives for Bubbles:

Each child will be able to:

1. Match the letter "B" with the word "bubble" and vice versa.
2. Summarize the read-aloud story in chronological order.
3. Give examples of how bubbles are used in everyday life.

Introductory Activity: Giant Bubble

Materials:

- toddler's wading pool
- large hoola hoop
- bottle of high-quality dishwashing detergent
- bottle of glycerine (it may be purchased at a pharmacy)
- bath towel
- several bricks

Preparation:

Place the pool in the middle of the floor. Place the towel in the middle of the pool and put several bricks on top of the towel. Add the dishwashing detergent and glycerine. Put about three inches of water into the tub. Place a hoola hoop in the water.

Procedure:

Have a student step on the bricks, swish the hoola hoop, and quickly lift the hoop around him- or herself—surrounding him- or herself with a bubble!

Recommended Books

***Bath Time for John* by Bob Graham** (Boston: Little Brown & Company, 1985); full-color illustrations; Interest Level: K-3; Reading Level: 1.8.

A toddler named John is taking a bath when his dog absconds with John's tub toy.

***Just Me in the Tub* by Gina and Mercer Mayer** (Racine, WI: Western Publishing Company, 1994); full-color illustrations; Interest Level: K-3; Reading Level: 1.8.

A little monster contends with the fun and clutter of a bath.

***King Bidgood's in the Bathtub* by Audrey Wood, illustrated by Don Wood** (San Diego, CA: Harcourt Brace Jovanovich, 1985); full-color illustrations; Interest Level: K-3; Reading Level: 1.6.

Despite their best efforts, no one can get King Bidgood out of the bathtub. No one, that is, except a young page.

***The Magic Bubble Trip* by Ingrid and Dieter Schubert** (New York: Kane/Miller Book Publishers, 1985); full-color illustrations; Interest Level: K-3; Reading Level: 3.4.

A magic bubble carries a young boy to a land of large, hairy frogs.

***Monster Bubbles: A Counting Book* by Dennis Nolan** (Englewood Cliffs, NJ: Prentice-Hall, 1976); two-color illustrations; Interest Level: K-3; Reading Level: 1.6.

Humorous monsters introduce the numerals one to ten by blowing bubbles.

Mortimer Mooner Stopped Taking a Bath **by Frank B. Edwards, illustrated by John Bianchi** (Newburgh, Ontario: Bungalo Books, 1990); full-color illustrations; Interest Level: K-3; Reading Level: 2.9.

A young pig stops practicing all personal hygiene until his grandmother motivates him to begin again.

Soap and Suds **by Diane Peterson** (New York: Alfred A. Knopf, 1984); full-color illustrations; Interest Level: K-3; Reading Level: 1.6.

A washerwoman, trying to wash her laundry, tries to cope with humorous interruptions.

To Bathe a Boa **by C. Imbior Kudrna** (Minneapolis: Carolrhoda Books, 1986); full-color illustrations; Interest Level: K-3; Reading Level: 2.5.

A boy tries every trick he knows to lure his pet snake into the bathtub.

The Tub People **by Pam Conrad, illustrated by Richard Egielski** (New York: HarperCollins, 1989); full-color illustrations; Interest Level: K-3; Reading Level: 3.5.

A toy figurine loses, then finds, his family when he is stuck in a bathtub drain.

Tubtime **by Elvira Woodruff, illustrated by Sucie Stevenson** (New York: Holiday House, 1990); full-color illustrations; Interest Level: K-3; Reading Level: 2.1.

Three little girls in a bathtub blow chickens, frogs, and alligators from their magic bubble pipes.

Nonfiction Resources

Easy to Make Water Toys that Really Work **by Mary Blocksma and Dewey Blocksma, illustrated by Art Seiden** (New York: Simon & Schuster, 1985); black-and-white illustrations; Interest Level: 3-6; Reading Level: 2.9.

Presents imaginative toys and illustrated instructions for making them using common materials.

I Wonder Why Soap Makes Bubbles and Other Questions About Science **by Barbara Taylor** (New York: Kingfisher, 1993); full-color illustrations; Interest Level: K-3; Reading Level: 4.5.

Poses and answers 31 questions about science and suggests experiments to prove the veracity of the explanations.

Rub-a-Dub-Dub Science in the Tub **by James Lewis, Illustrated by Joe Greenwald** (New York: Meadowbrook Press, 1989); black-and-white illustrations; Interest Level: K-3; Reading Level: not listed.

Contains 33 experiments to introduce toddlers and preschoolers to basic scientific concepts.

Soap Bubble Magic **by Seymour Simon, illustrated by Stella Ormai** (New York: Lothrop, Lee & Shepard, 1985); two-color illustrations; Interest Level: K-3; Reading Level: 2.3.

Presents soap experiments, suggests observations students should make during the experiments, and applies those observations to our physical world.

Tom Noddy's Bubble Magic **by Tom Noddy** (Philadelphia: Running Press, 1988); black/white photographs and illustrations; Interest Level: 3-6; Reading Level: 6.8.

Noddy demonstrates, step by step, how to create many unusual bubble shapes.

Recipe: Bubble Punch

1 12-ounce can ginger ale

1 10-ounce container orange/pineapple juice

4 scoops sherbet, any flavor

This recipe makes four servings. Place one scoop of sherbet in each of four 9-ounce cups. Equally divide the ginger ale and juice into each cup.

Music Activity: "Bubbles, Bubbles"

The accompanying finger plays follow the song.

BUBBLES, BUBBLES (Sung to the tune "Old MacDonald.")

B– U– B– B– L– E– S,   Bub–bles ev– ery

where.   Tooth–paste bub–bles   in   my   mouth,

Sham–poo in my   hair.   With a   bub–ble bub–ble here and a

bub–ble bub–ble there.   Rub–a–dub, Scrub–a–dub,   bub–bles in the bath–tub.

B– U– B– B– L– E– S,   Bub–bles ev– ery   where.

     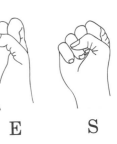

B U B B L E S

Bubbles

every

where.

Toothpaste

bubbles

in

my

mouth,

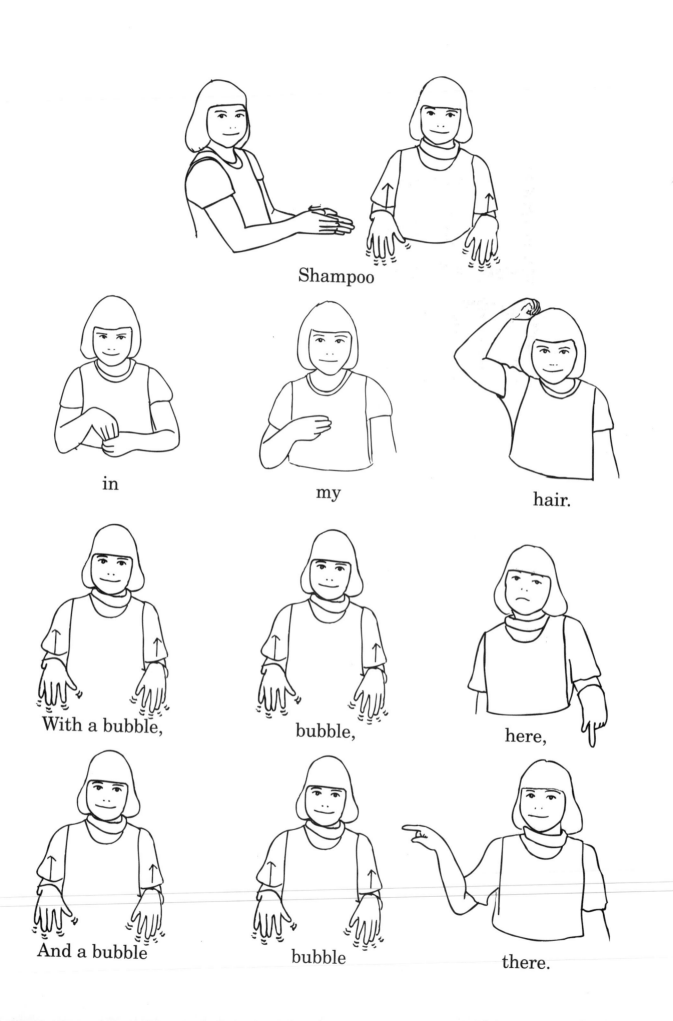

Shampoo

in

my

hair.

With a bubble,

bubble,

here,

And a bubble

bubble

there.

Rub-a-dub,

Scrub-a-dub,

Bubbles

in

the bath

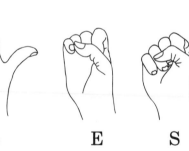

tub.

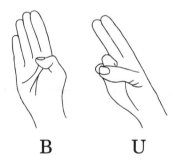

B　　U　　B　　B　　L　　E　　S

Bubbles

every

where.

Art Activity: Bubble Creature

Materials:

- inflated balloons (one balloon per child)
- stickers in various shapes, sizes, and colors
- balloon bases cut from construction paper or posterboard using the pattern on the following page (one base per child)
- scissors
- 8-1/2-inch square of cardboard to serve as a template
- paper punch
- pencil or pen

Preparation:

Inflate balloons and tie off the ends. Cut out the balloon base pattern and trace the shape onto posterboard or construction paper. Cut out the bases, cutting a hole with a paper punch where indicated on the template.

Directions:

Have students insert the end of their balloon through the hole in the balloon base so that the balloon stands upright. Have students decorate their balloons with the stickers.

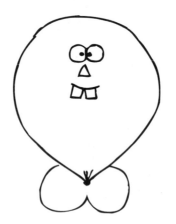

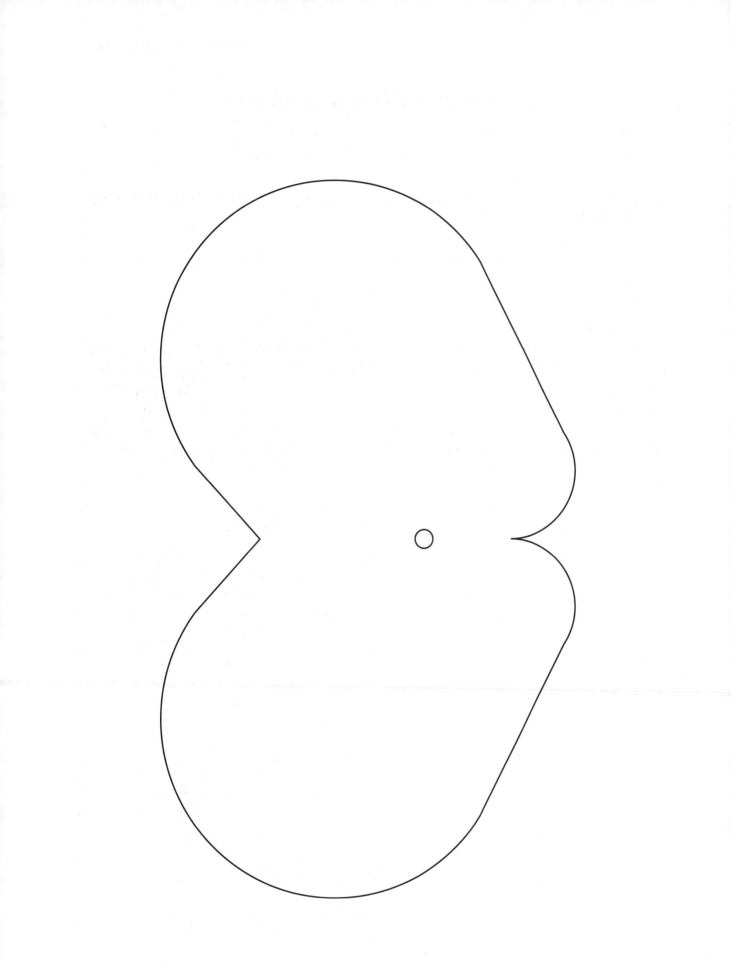

Pattern for Balloon Base

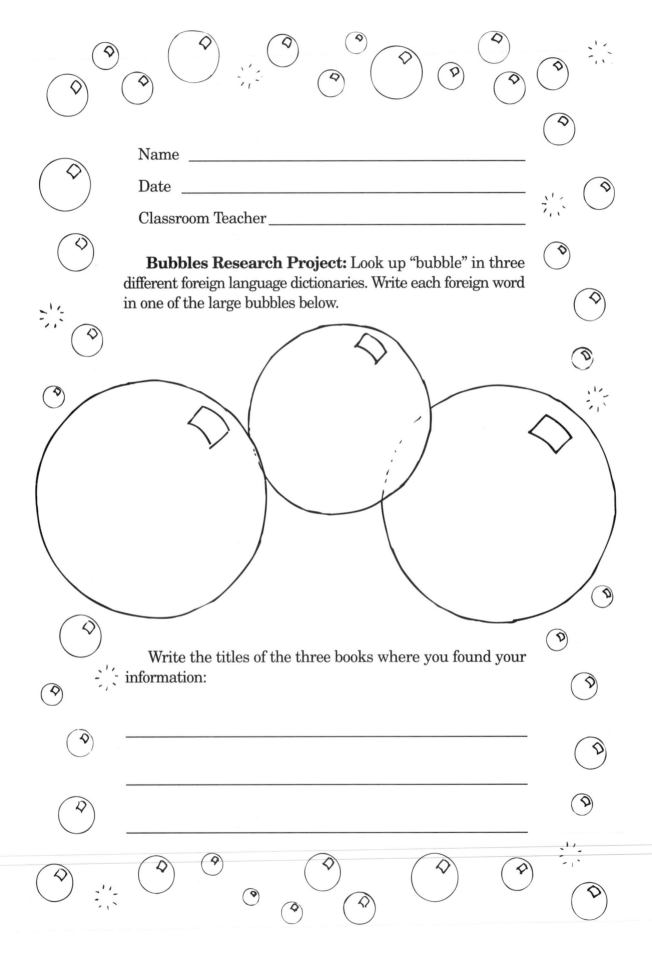

Name _____

Date _____

Classroom Teacher _____

Bubbles Research Project: Look up "bubble" in three different foreign language dictionaries. Write each foreign word in one of the large bubbles below.

Write the titles of the three books where you found your information:

_____

_____

_____

Camping

Getting Ready to Teach the Letter C

Set the mood for this lesson by building a "campfire" in the middle of the library floor. Place one or more night lights on the floor, running an electric extension cord to the nearest outlet. (If you are dealing with very young children, use battery-operated flashlights.) Stack several logs around the night lights and turn off all overhead lights. Also play an audio tape of forest sounds. (I recommend *Walk Through the Forest* available from The Madacy Music Group Inc., P.O. Box 1445, St. Laurent, Quebec, Canada H4L 4Z1.) Later, after the students have assembled around the campfire, hand each child a marshmallow on a long straw and give them a few minutes to "roast" their marshmallows over the campfire.

Objectives for Camping:

Each student will be able to:

1. Match the letter "C" with the word "camping" and vice versa.

2. Summarize the read-aloud story in chronological order.

3. Identify the animals that live in a forest.

Introductory Activity: Animal Tracks Flash Cards

Materials:

- photocopies of the animal tracks cards

Preparation:

Photocopy and, if necessary, enlarge the animal track flash cards.

Procedure:

Hold up each card and have students guess which animal made the tracks. It may be necessary to give the children clues about each animal as the guessing progresses. (Card 1: duck; Card 2: deer; Card 3: rabbit; Card 4: bear; Card 5: raccoon; Card 6: human.)

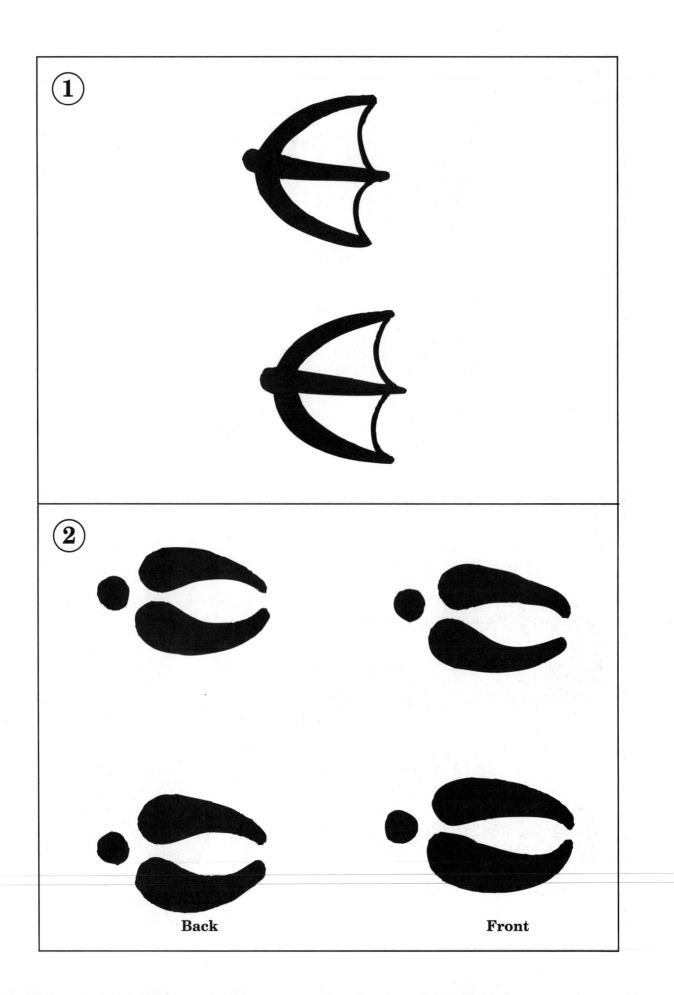

②

Back   **Front**

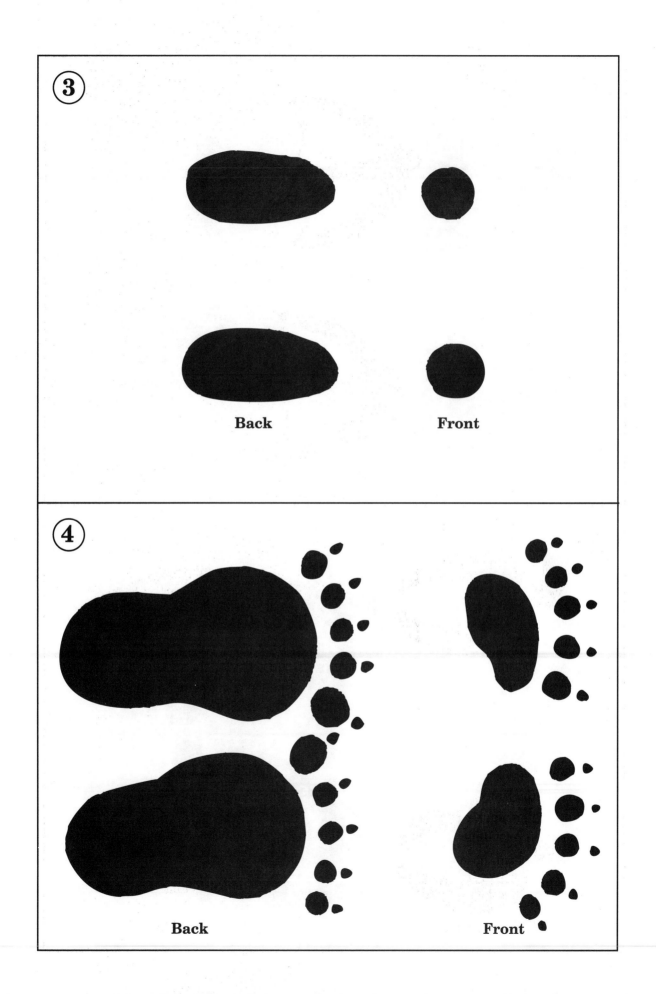

③

Back   Front

④

Back   Front

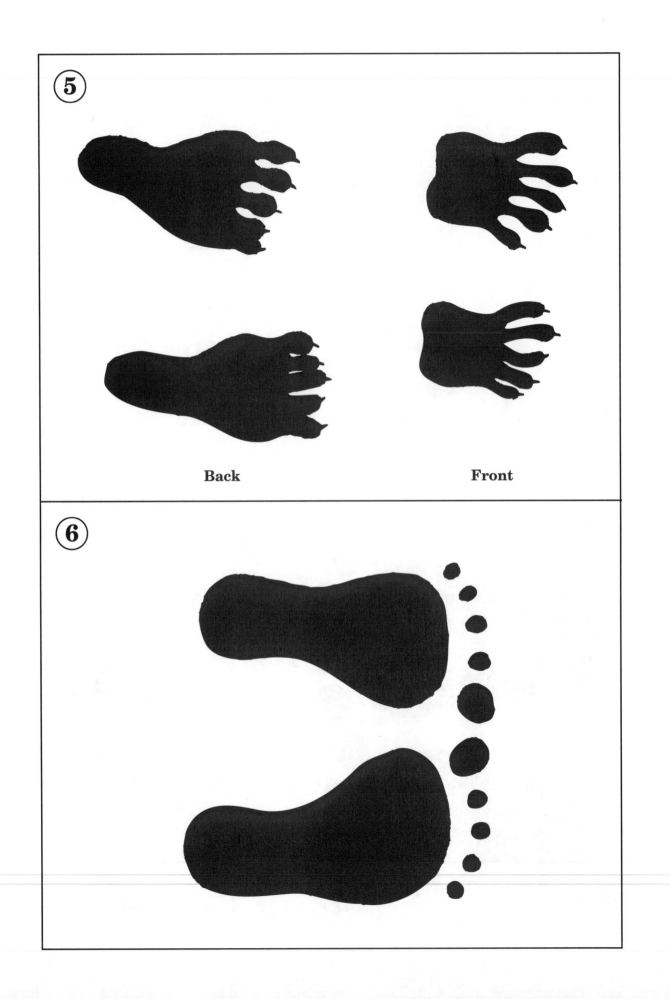

Back

Front

Recommended Books

***Amelia Bedelia Goes Camping* by Peggy Parish, illustrated by Lynn Sweat** (New York: Greenwillow, 1985); three-color illustrations; Interest Level: K-3; Reading Level: 1.5.

A whacky maid named Amelia Bedelia creates havoc when she misinterprets her employer's camping instructions.

***Bear* by John Schoenherr** (New York: Philomel Books, 1991); full-color illustrations; Interest Level: K-3; Reading Level: 4.6.

A young orphaned bear learns to survive and later thrive in the northern wilderness.

***The Berenstain Bears Blaze a Trail* by Stan and Jan Berenstain** (New York: Random House; 1987); full-color illustrations; Interest Level: K-3; Reading Level: 3.0.

A misguided Papa Bear takes his scout cubs for a nature walk where his lack of hiking skills becomes readily apparent.

***Blueberries for Sal* by Robert McCloskey** (New York: Puffin Books, 1948); blue-and-white illustrations; Interest Level: K-3; Reading Level: 3.8.

A little girl, picking blueberries in the country with her mother, inadvertently wanders off with a mother bear who is searching for her cub.

***Deep in the Forest* by Brinton Turkle** (New York: Puffin Unicorn, 1976); brown-wash illustrations; Interest Level: K-3; No words.

A bear cub, following the pattern of Goldilocks, breaks into a cabin and samples the bowls of food, the chairs, and the beds—until the family returns home and chases the bear cub home!

***Do Not Disturb* by Nancy Tafuri** (New York: Greenwillow Books, 1987); full-color illustrations; Interest Level: K-3; No words.

A family, camping in the woods, affects the lives of the animals living there.

***In the Forest* written and illustrated by Marie Hall Ets** (New York: Penguin, 1944); black-and-white illustrations; Interest Level: K-3; Reading Level: 3.6.

A young boy goes for a walk in the forest and imagines he is leading a parade of animals.

***Keep Looking* by Millicent Selsan and Joyce Hunt, illustrated by Normand Chartier** (New York: Macmillan, 1989); full-color illustrations; Interest Level: K-3; Reading Level: 2.0.

Forest animals visit a country home in winter. The reader is encouraged to find and identify various animals in the illustrations.

***Pig Pig Goes to Camp* by David McPhail** (New York: Dutton, 1983); full-color illustrations; Interest Level: K-3; Reading Level: 3.9.

Pig Pig enjoys his summer camp experience and takes special pleasure in his new-found friendship with the local frog population.

***Wild Critters* by Tim Jones, photography by Tom Walker** (Fairbanks, AK: Epicenter Press/Graphic Arts Center, 1992); full-color photos; Interest Level: K-3; Reading Level: 2.9.

Contains humorous verses and photographs of twenty Alaskan wild animals.

Nonfiction Resources

***Animal Tracks* written and illustrated by Arthur Dorros** (New York: Scholastic, 1991); full-color illustrations; Interest Level: K-3; Reading Level: 3.3.

The author introduces the ecosystem of a riverbank through the animals that laid their tracks there.

***In My Tent* by Marilyn Singer, illustrated by Emily Arnold McCully** (New York: Macmillan, 1992); full-color illustrations; Interest Level: K-3; Reading Level: 5.5.

A series of poems documents a child's first camping trip.

***Nature Walk* by Douglas Florian** (New York: Greenwillow, 1989); full-color illustrations; Interest Level: K-3; Reading Level: 1.3.

Two children walk through the woods exploring the flora and fauna.

***North Country Night* by Daniel San Souci** (New York: Doubleday 1990); full-color illustrations; Interest Level: K-3; Reading Level: 3.4.

Describes the nocturnal animals on a winter night in the North Country.

***Who Lives in the Forest?* by Ron Hirschi, photographs by Galen Burrell** (New York: Dodd Mead & Co., 1987); full-color photographs; Interest Level: K-3; Reading Level: 2.7.

Vivid photographs identify forest animals and introduce readers to their interrelated lives.

Recipe: No-Cook S'mores

1 package graham crackers*

1 7-ounce jar marshmallow sandwich spread

5 chocolate candy bars

This recipe makes ten s'mores. Break graham cracker rectangles into squares. Spread marshmallow sandwich spread on half of the graham cracker squares. Place one half chocolate bar on top of marshmallow square and top with another graham cracker square.

*One package of graham crackers contains ten graham crackers. A 64-ounce box of graham crackers contains three such packages.

Music Activity: "We Took a Walk in the Woods"

This song can be signed in American Sign Language. (The movements to use are given following the song.) The leader sings and signs the first verse to one of the students. The student replies by naming a forest animal. The leader then demonstrates how to sign the identified animal and sings and signs the second verse, substituting the animal in the blanks. Continue singing the second verse to different students, substituting the identified animals and encouraging students to sign the song with the leader.

WE TOOK A WALK IN THE WOODS
(Sung to the tune "The Bear Went Over the Mountain.")

Verse 2

We saw a *(animal 1)* in the woods,
We saw a *(animal 1)* in the woods,
We saw a *(animal 1)* in the woods,
And we also saw a *(animal 2)*.

Repeat lines 1 and 2 three times.

Line 1   We

Line 2   took a walk   in the   woods.

Line 3   And what   do   you

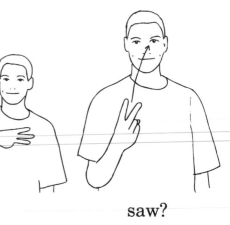

Line 4   think   we   saw?

Repeat lines 5 and 6 three times.

Line 5   We   saw

Line 6   <u>   </u> a ***   in the   woods.

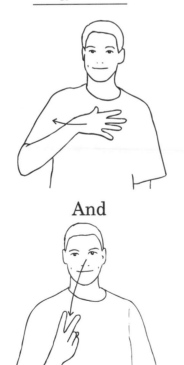 

Line 7   And   we

Line 8   also saw   a ***<u>   </u>.

*** Please refer to the following page for sign language to represent various forest animals.

Deer

Owl

Squirrel

Skunk

Fox

Art Activity: Wild Animal Bookmarks

Materials:
- photocopies of the bookmarks
- crayons
- safety scissors

Preparation:

Photocopy the bookmarks, making one copy for each child.

Procedure:

Have students color and cut out their bookmarks.

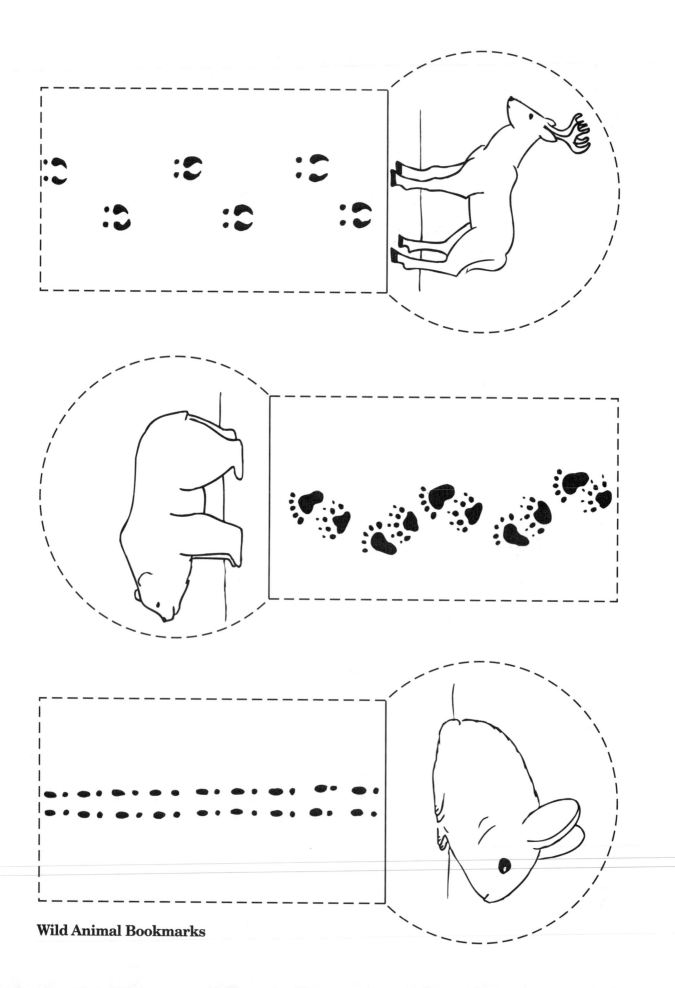

Wild Animal Bookmarks

Name _____

Date _____

Classroom Teacher _____

Camping Research Project: Look up "national parks" in an almanac or other reference source. Write the names of three different national parks in the trees below.

Write the title of the book where you found your information.

_____

_____

Dinosaurs

Getting Ready to Teach the Letter D

Dinosaurs are very popular with the preschool and primary age groups. Encourage children to bring their dinosaur objects, clearly marked with the children's names, to the library for a fascinating display.

Objectives for Dinosaurs:

Each student will be able to:

1. Match the letter "D" with the word "dinosaur" and vice versa.

2. Summarize the read-aloud story in chronological order.

3. Name several species of dinosaurs.

Introductory Activity: Dinosaur Drawing Story

Today I'm going to tell you a story. I'll make an "S" for story.

This is a story about *(child's name)*. One evening, *(child's name)* was walking in his/her backyard when he/she thought he/she saw something. When he/she rubbed his/her eyes and looked again, though, it was gone. So *(child's name)* started to look for it.

First, *(child's name)* looked behind the fence, but it wasn't there.

Then *(child's name)* walked to the pond. *(Child's name)* looked around the pond...

But all *(child's name)* saw was a stick and a turtle in the pond. *(Child's name)* kept walking.

(Child's name) looked behind a tree stump, but saw nothing.

(Child's name) kept walking until he/she had reached the length of his/her yard.

(Child's name) never again saw what he/she thought he/she saw in his/her backyard. Can you guess what *(child's name)* saw in his/her backyard? A dimetrodon dinosaur!

Recommended Books

***An Alphabet of Dinosaurs* by Peter Dodson, paintings by Wayne D. Barlowe, illustrations by Michael Meaker** (Los Angeles: A Byron Press Visual Publications Book; 1995); full-color and black-and-white illustrations; Interest Level: K-3; Reading Level: 2.9.

Dramatic illustrations and informative text name and describe dinosaurs from A to Z.

***The Berenstain Bears and the Missing Dinosaur Bone* by Stan and Jan Berenstain** (New York: Random House, 1980); full-color illustrations; Interest Level: K-3; Reading Level: 2.9.

In this rhyming story, three small bear detectives search a natural history museum for a missing dinosaur bone.

***Bones, Bones, Dinosaur Bones* by Bryon Barton** (New York: Thomas Y. Crowell, 1990); full-color illustrations; Interest Level: K-3; Reading Level: 1.4.

Simple text and illustrations describe the work of archaeologists as they find dinosaur bones and assemble them at the natural history museum.

***Dad's Dinosaur Day* by Diane Dawson Hearn** (New York: Macmillan, 1993); full-color illustrations; Interest Level: K-3; Reading Level: 1.7.

A young boy, waking to find his father has turned into a dinosaur, spends the day with him romping and playing.

***The Dinosaur Who Lived in My Backyard* by B.G. Hennessy, illustrated by Susan Davis** (New York: Puffin Books, 1988); full-color illustrations; Interest Level: K-3; Reading Level: 3.3.

The author uses fanciful dinosaurs in a modern-day setting to explain basic concepts about dinosaurs.

***The Foolish Dinosaur Fiasco* by Scott Corbett, illustrated by Jon McIntosh** (Boston: Little Brown & Company, 1978); two-color illustrations; Interest Level: 3-6; Reading Level: 3.8.

A boy named Nick and his dog enter an amusement park where Dr. Merlin forces them to become dinosaur trainers.

***Katie and the Dinosaurs* by James Mayhew** (New York: Bantam Little Rooster, 1992); full-color illustrations; Interest Level: K-3; Reading Level: 4.9.

A little girl walks into a restricted room in the natural history museum and enters a world of live dinosaurs.

***Mrs. Toggle and the Dinosaurs* by Robin Pulver, illustrated by R.W. Alley** (New York: Aladdin Paperbacks, 1995); full-color illustrations; Interest Level: K-3; Reading Level: 3.3.

Mrs. Toggle and her class prepare their school for the arrival of a new student whom they believe to be a dinosaur.

***Tyrannosaurus Tex* by Betty G. Birney, illustrated by John O'Brien** (Boston: Houghton Mifflin, 1994); full-color illustrations; Interest Level: K-3; Reading Level: 2.3.

A friendly cowboy dinosaur joins a cattle drive and saves the day when rustlers start a fire.

***What Happened to Patrick's Dinosaurs?* by Carol Carrick, illustrated by Donald Carrick** (New York: Clarion Books, 1986); full-color illustrations; Interest Level: K-3; Reading Level: 2.8.

Two brothers, Patrick and Hank, imagine a time when dinosaurs and people lived together and what happened when the dinosaurs left.

Nonfiction Resources

Be a Dinosaur Detective **by Dougal Dixon** (New York: Lerner, 1987); full-color illustrations; Interest Level: K-3; Reading Level: 4.7.

Large, lavish illustrations and text show various dinosaurs, their skeletal features, and the formation of fossils.

The Day of the Dinosaur **by Stan and Jan Berenstain, illustrated by Michael Berenstain** (New York: Random House, 1987); full-color illustrations; Interest Level: K-3; Reading Level: 2.7.

Colorful illustrations and brief text introduce familiar dinosaur species.

Dinosaur Bones **by Aliki** (New York: Harper & Row, 1988); full-color illustrations; Interest Level: K-3; Reading Level: 4.9.

This book explains how dinosaurs are classified.

Dinosaurs **by Gail Gibbons** (New York: Holiday House, 1987); full-color illustrations; Interest Level: K-3; Reading Level: 3.5.

Brief text introduces the youngest readers to the different types of dinosaurs.

Dinosaurs, Dinosaurs **by Byron Barton** (New York: Thomas Y. Crowell; 1989); full-color illustrations; Interest Level: K-3; Reading Level: 1.6.

Describes the physical features of various dinosaurs.

My First Pop-Up Book of Dinosaurs **by Roma Bishop, designed by Graham Brown and Ruth Mawdsley** (New York: Simon & Schuster, 1993); full-color illustrations; Interest Level: K-3; Reading Level: Not listed.

Pop-up mechanics introduce children to six dinosaur species.

Recipe: Dinowiches

1 jar peanut butter

selection of jams and jellies

1 loaf sliced bread

sliced cheese

sliced cold cuts

Use sandwich fillings to make closed-face sandwiches. Use dinosaur-shaped cookie cutters to cut the sandwiches into dinosaur shapes. Dinosaur cookie cutters are available from: Ekco, Franklin Park, IL **or** Fox Run, Ivyland, PA.

Music Activity: "Dinosaur Song"

You will need a small plastic dinosaur or a small picture of a dinosaur for this game (see the dinosaur pattern on the following page). First, teach the class the song. Then choose someone to be "IT." Have IT leave the classroom and hide the dinosaur in the classroom. When IT returns, begin continuously singing the song. IT is to find the dinosaur; when IT is close to the dinosaur, the class will sing loudly. When IT is far away from the dinosaur, sing softly. Continue singing until IT has located the dinosaur.

DINOSAUR SONG (Sung to the tune "Go Tell Aunt Rhody.")

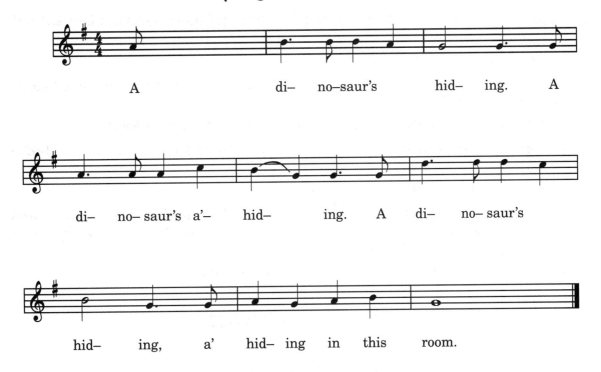

A   di— no—saur's   hid— ing.   A

di— no— saur's a'— hid—   ing.   A di— no— saur's

hid—   ing,   a' hid— ing in this   room.

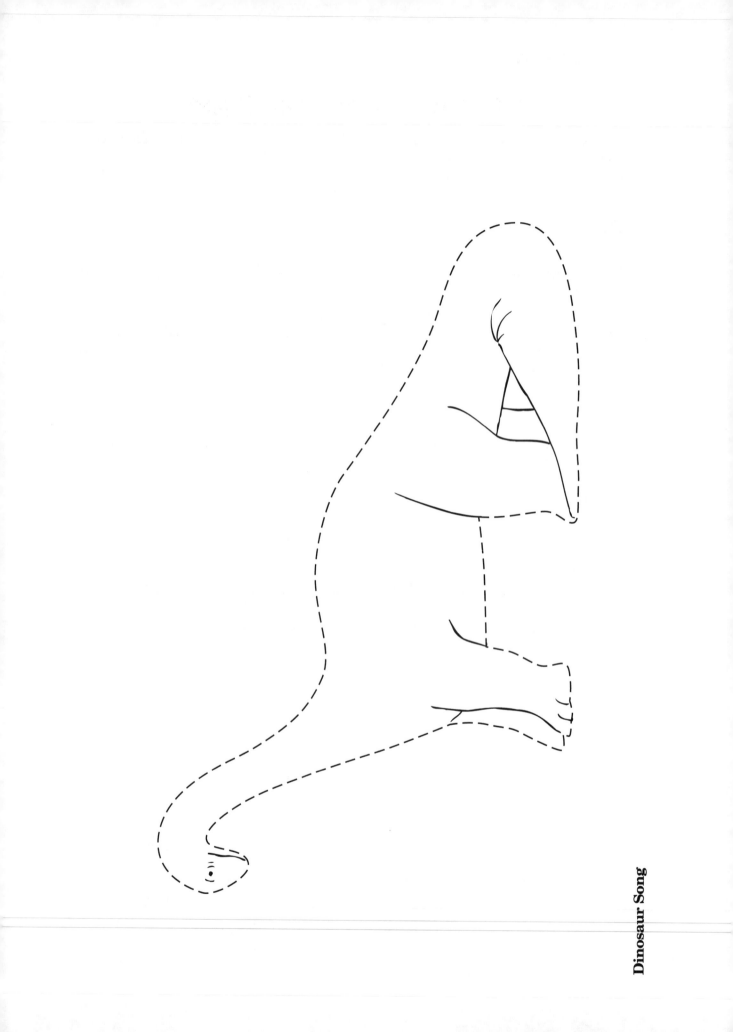

Dinosaur Song

Art Activity: Dinosaur Finger Puppet

Materials:

- photocopies of the dinosaur finger puppet pattern
- crayons
- safety scissors
- X-acto™ knife

Preparation:

Photocopy the dinosaur pattern, making one copy per child. Use an X-acto™ knife to cut the two marked slits in the middle of the dinosaur.

Procedure:

Have students color and cut out the dinosaur. Show students how to place the strip of paper in the middle of the dinosaur under their forefinger to create a finger puppet. By slowly raising and lowering their arm, the students can make the puppet flap its wings.

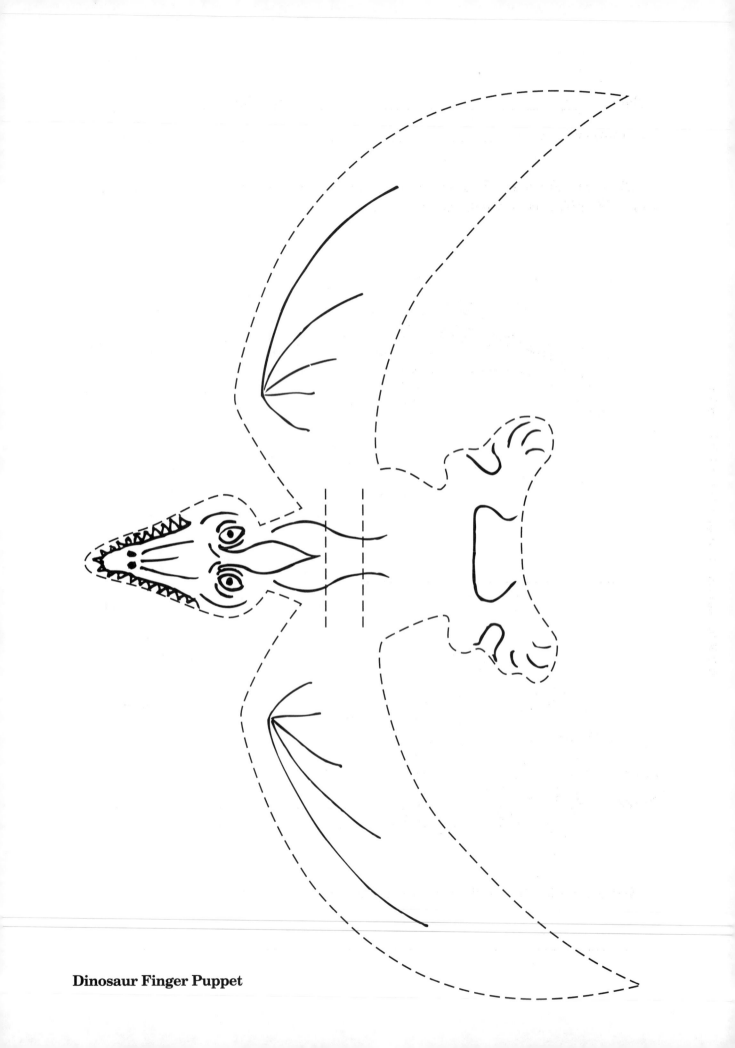

Dinosaur Finger Puppet

Name _____ Date _____

Classroom Teacher _____

Dinosaurs Research Project: Look up "dinosaur" in an encyclopedia or other reference source. Identify each of the dinosaurs below.

_____

_____

_____

Write the title of the book where you found your information:

_____

Eggs

Getting Ready to Teach the Letter E

If possible, prepare for this unit by visiting a local county fair with a microphone and tape recorder and recording the sounds inside the poultry pavilion. If this is not feasible, banjo music also sets a country mood. ("Dueling Banjos: The Best of the Banjo" is available from Highland Music, Dearborn, MI 48126.) Dress in overalls and a farmer's hat and carry a basket of plastic chicken eggs. If the group is small, you might want to break a real chicken egg in a bowl and point out the shell, yolk, egg white, chalaza, and germ.

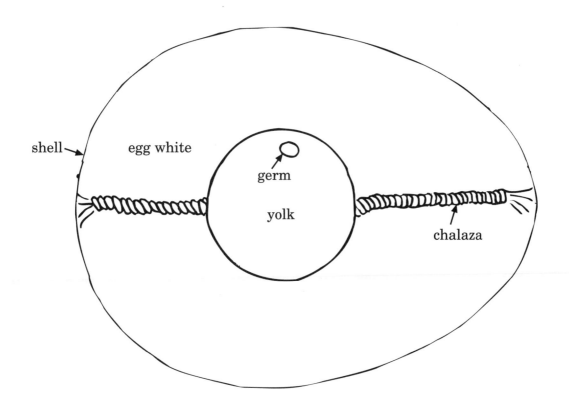

Objectives for Eggs:

Each student will be able to:

1. Match the letter "E" with the word "egg" and vice versa.

2. Summarize the read-aloud story in chronological order.

3. List animals that hatch from eggs.

Introductory Activity: Egg Poem Riddles

Materials:

- photocopies of six "cracked egg" patterns and accompanying poems with illustrations
- crayons, markers, or colored pencils
- scissors

Preparation:

Photocopy six copies of the "cracked egg" pattern. Cut out the eggs along the solid lines. Cut out the animal pictures and riddle poems. Use markers, crayons or colored pencils to color the animal pictures. Glue an animal picture in the middle of the egg and the corresponding riddle on the back of the egg. Repeat for each animal and riddle poem. Close the two flaps over each egg on the broken lines to create a "cracked egg" that hides the animal inside the egg.

Procedure:

Explain to the children that you are going to read them a poem and they must determine the last word to the poem. Read one of the poems to the class and when the students correctly determine the missing word, open the flaps to reveal the corresponding picture. Repeat the procedure for the other eggs.

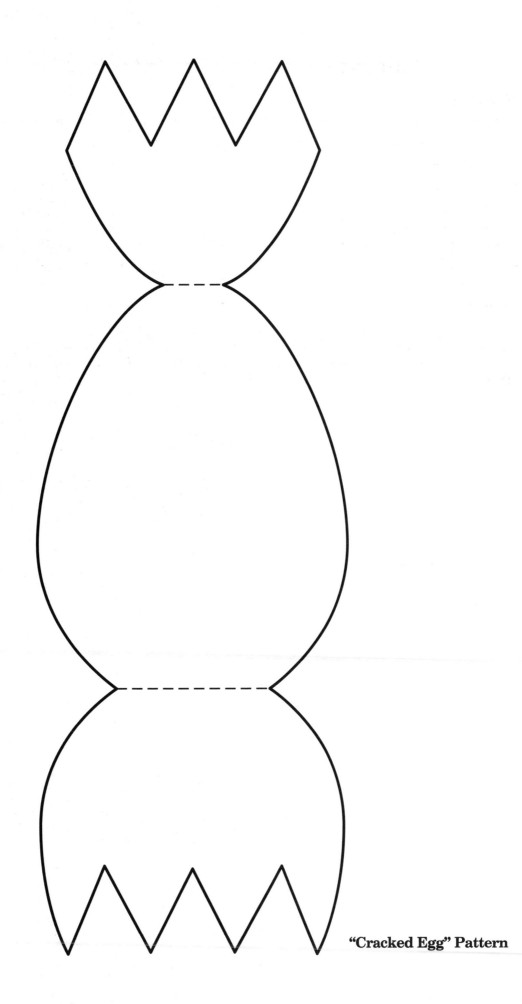

"Cracked Egg" Pattern

My dinosaur egg,
Is large and quite complex.
My teeth are sharp and ferocious,
They call me tyrannosaurus *(rex)*.

My egg was laid in a swamp,
And I hatched nine weeks later.
I can grow twelve feet long.
I am an *(alligator)*.

My egg was in a honeycomb,
In a tall apple tree.
I work for my queen now,
As a buzzing worker *(bee)*.

I hatched from an egg,
Though it looked quite absurd.
I have feathers and a beak.
They call me a *(bird)*.

When I was an egg,
I had just one wish,
To swim in the ocean,
As a beautiful *(fish)*.

My egg was laid,
In a pond near a log.
I hatched into a tadpole,
And grew into a *(frog)*.

Recommended Books

***Bently & Egg* written and illustrated by William Joyce** (New York: HarperCollins, 1992); full-color illustrations; Interest Level: K-3; Reading Level: 5.7.

A shy frog named Bently bravely rescues and protects an egg that hatches into a duckling.

***The Big Bunny and the Easter Egg* by Steven Kroll, illustrated by Janet Stevens** (New York: Scholastic, 1988); full-color illustrations; Interest Level: K-3; Reading Level: 2.0.

Loyal rabbit friends help Wilbur, the Easter Bunny, deliver Easter baskets when he develops a bad cold.

***An Extraordinary Egg* by Leo Lionni** (New York: Knopf, 1994); full-color illustrations; Interest Level: K-3; Reading Level: 3.5.

Three humorous frogs discover an alligator egg. When it hatches, the frogs believe the baby alligator is a chick.

***Green Eggs and Ham* by Dr. Seuss** (New York: Random House; 1960, 1988); four-color illustrations; Interest Level: K-3; Reading Level: 2.2.

Sam tries to convince a stubborn curmudgeon to sample his green eggs and ham.

***Happy Easter, Grandma* by Harriet Ziefert, illustrated by Sidney Levitt** (New York: Harper & Row, 1988); full-color illustrations; Interest Level: K-3; Reading Level: not listed.

Rabbit searches for, and eventually finds, a perfect Easter egg for his grandmother.

***Horton Hatches the Egg* by Dr. Seuss** (New York: Random House, 1940); two-color illustrations; Interest Level: K-3; Reading Level: 3.6.

In this rhyming tale, an elephant named Horton sits on an egg waiting for it to hatch, despite many adversities.

***Ida and Betty and the Secret Eggs* by Kay Chorea** (New York: Clarion Books, 1991); full-color illustrations; Interest Level: K-3; Reading Level: 4.9.

Two best friends, Ida and Betty, share the fun of waiting for four robin eggs to hatch until Lucinda, the new neighbor, lures Betty away from Ida and their secret project.

***Just Plain Fancy* written and illustrated by Patricia Polacca** (New York: Bantam, 1990); full-color illustrations; Interest Level: K-3; Reading Level: 3.8.

Two Amish girls, who live lives of strict simplicity, are perplexed when a "fancy" egg appears at their farm and eventually hatches into a peacock.

***The Most Wonderful Egg in the World* written and illustrated by Helme Heine** (New York: Atheneum, 1983); full-color illustrations; Interest Level: K-3; Reading Level: 3.5.

Three hens compete before the king to lay the most wonderful egg.

***Seven Eggs* by Meredith Hooper, illustrated by Terry McKenna** (New York: Harper & Row, 1985); color illustrations; Interest Level: K-3; Reading Level: not listed.

In this lift-the-flap book, six different eggs hatch six different animals. The seventh egg contains a surprise.

Nonfiction Resources

***Chickens Aren't the Only Ones* by Ruth Heller** (New York: Grosset & Dunlap, 1981); full-color illustrations; Interest Level: K-3; Reading Level: 3.6.

Vibrant illustrations and rhyming text present the many animals that lay eggs.

***The Egg: A First Discovery Book* by Gallimard Jeunesse and Pascale de Bourgoing, illustrated by Rene Mettler** (New York: Scholastic, 1989); full-color illustrations; Interest Level: K-3; Reading Level: 2.7.

Transparent pages show the internal development of a chicken egg and identify other animals that also lay eggs.

***Egg Story* by Anca Hariton** (New York: Dutton Children's Books, 1992); full-color illustrations; Interest Level: K-3; Reading Level: 3.9.

Describes the cycle of a chicken egg from the time it is laid to the time it is hatched.

***Eggshells to Objects: A New Approach to Egg Craft* by Susan Riser Arnold** (New York: Holt, Rinehart, and Winston, 1979); full-color illustrations; Interest Level: 5-8; Reading Level: 5.2.

Presents instructions to create over 30 easy projects using eggshells.

***Egg-ventures: First Science Experiments* by Harry Milgrom, illustrated by Giulio Maestro** (New York: E.P. Dutton & Co., 1974); two-color illustrations; Interest Level: K-3; Reading Level: not listed.

Presents step-by-step instructions for easy experiments to introduce children to basic scientific concepts.

Recipe: Bird's Nest Salad

1 6-ounce can of tuna fish	1/3 cup mayonnaise
1/2 cup finely chopped celery	1/8 teaspoon salt
2 firm apples, peeled and finely cut	1 head of lettuce, separated into leaves
3 hard-boiled eggs, shelled	

This recipe makes six servings. Separate the hard-boiled egg white from the egg yolk, taking care to keep the yolk whole. Chop the egg white and carefully cut the yolks in half. Reserve the yolks. Mix all of the ingredients except the yolks and lettuce leaves. Place a lettuce leaf on a salad plate and put a scoop of salad on the leaf. Hollow the center of the salad scoop to resemble a nest and place an egg yolk half in the center of the nest, flat side down, to resemble an egg. (*Optional:* Cover and chill for one hour before serving.)

Music Activity: "I Like Eggs"

The accompanying finger plays follow the song.

I LIKE EGGS (Sung to the tune "Three Blind Mice.")

I like eggs. I like

eggs. Nice, tast– y eggs.

Nice, tast– y eggs. I like them scram– bled, I

like them fried, creamed and cur– ried and poached and dyed,

shirred and cod– dled with ham on the side. Yes, I like eggs.

Finger Plays:

I like eggs, I like eggs.	*(Make a spherical shape with hands.)*
Nice, tasty eggs. Nice, tasty eggs.	*(Rub tummy.)*
I like them scrambled, I like them fried, creamed and curried and poached and dyed,	*(Pretend to stir eggs in a bowl.)*
Shirred and coddled with ham on the side.	*(Pretend to flip eggs in a pan.)*
Yes, I like eggs.	*(Rub tummy.)*

Art Project: Egg Surprise

Materials:

- photocopies of the "cracked egg" pattern used for the Egg Poem Riddles (Indtroductory Activity)
- crayons
- safety scissors

Preparation:

Photocopy the egg pattern, making one copy per child.

Procedure:

Have students cut out the egg, folding up the bottom section and down the top section to create a hinged cracked egg. Have students open the egg and draw a realistic or fanciful animal on the blank egg.

On the back of the egg, have children write poems or riddles about the animal they drew.

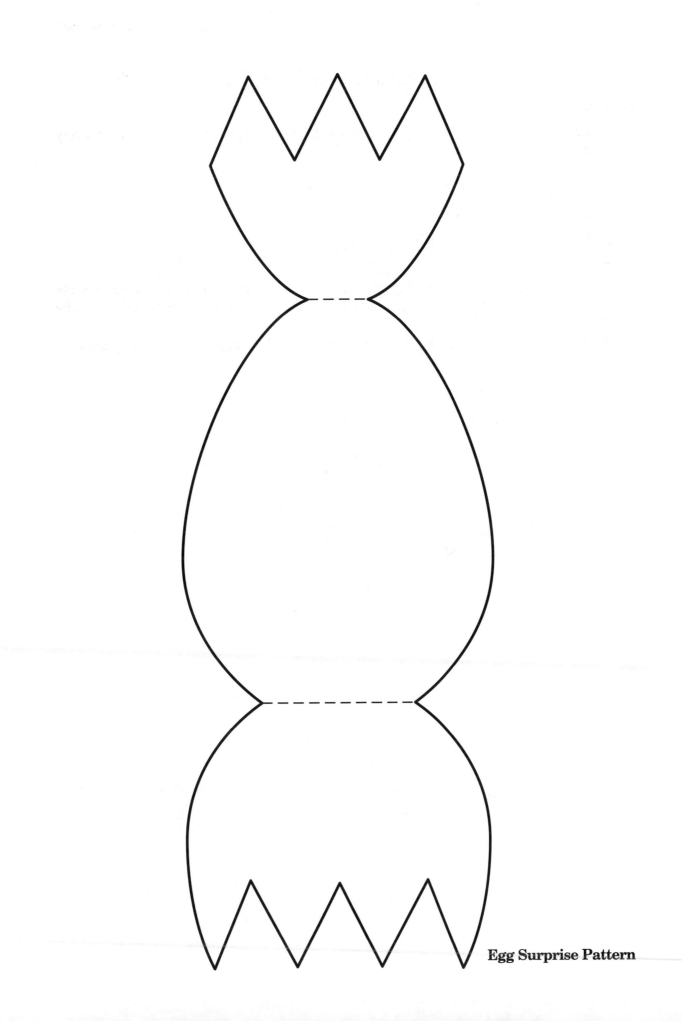

Egg Surprise Pattern

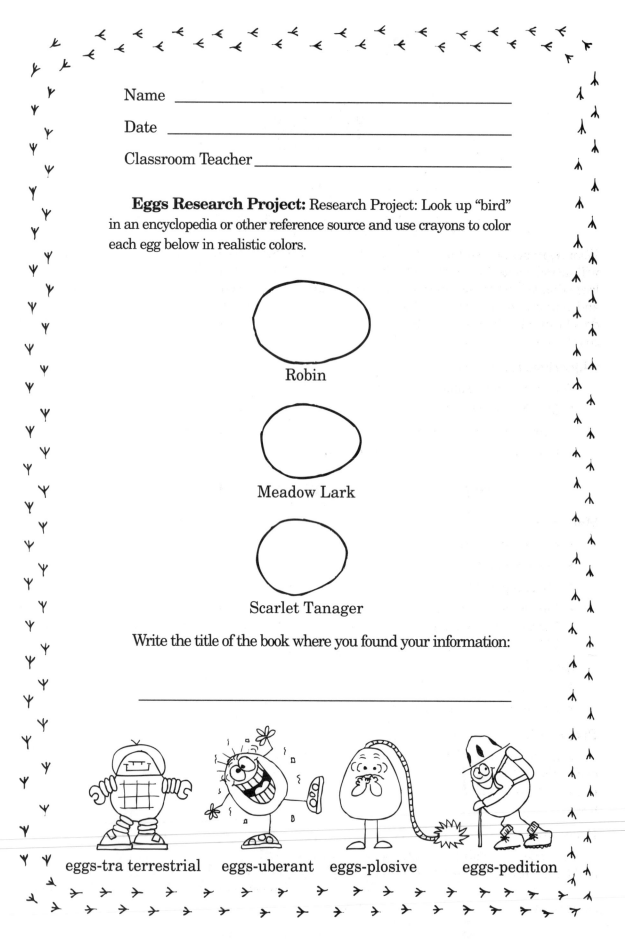

Name _____

Date _____

Classroom Teacher _____

Eggs Research Project: Research Project: Look up "bird" in an encyclopedia or other reference source and use crayons to color each egg below in realistic colors.

Robin

Meadow Lark

Scarlet Tanager

Write the title of the book where you found your information:

_____

eggs-tra terrestrial   eggs-uberant   eggs-plosive   eggs-pedition

Frogs

Getting Ready to Teach the Letter F

Wear a green sweatsuit to introduce the frog unit. Have a bowl of raisins near your desk that you will introduce as flies. Explain to the children that you have been reading so many books about frogs that you have noticed that your skin is turning green, you are strangely drawn to bathtubs, and you have developed a fondness for fly snacks (as you pop a few raisins in your mouth)! Next, do a brief talk about frog books available for circulation, but warn students about the possible consequences of reading such books!

Objectives for Frogs:

Each child will be able to:

1. Match the letter "F" with the word "frog" and vice versa.

2. Summarize the read-aloud story in chronological order.

3. Explain a frog's habitat, life cycle, and diet.

Introductory Activity: Musical Lily Pads

Materials:

- green construction paper
- scissors and tape
- lily pad pattern
- tape recorder and a musical audio tape (or an audio tape of frog sounds available from Northsound Audio, distributed by Holborne Distributing Co., Ltd., Mount Albert, ONT LOG 1MO.)

optional:

- a small prize
- a large blue or green sheet

Preparation:

Cut out the lily pad pattern. Trace onto green construction paper and cut out one lily pad for each child in the class. Tape a lily pad onto each library chair and arrange the chairs in a circle facing out. *Optional:* Place the chairs on a blue or green sheet and call the game area the "frog pond."

Procedure:

Arrange the children in front of the chairs and take away one chair. Begin playing the music and have the children walk in a circle around the chairs. When the music stops, every child is to sit in a chair. The one child who cannot find a chair stands to the side. The game continues in the same manner until one child remains, who is the winner.

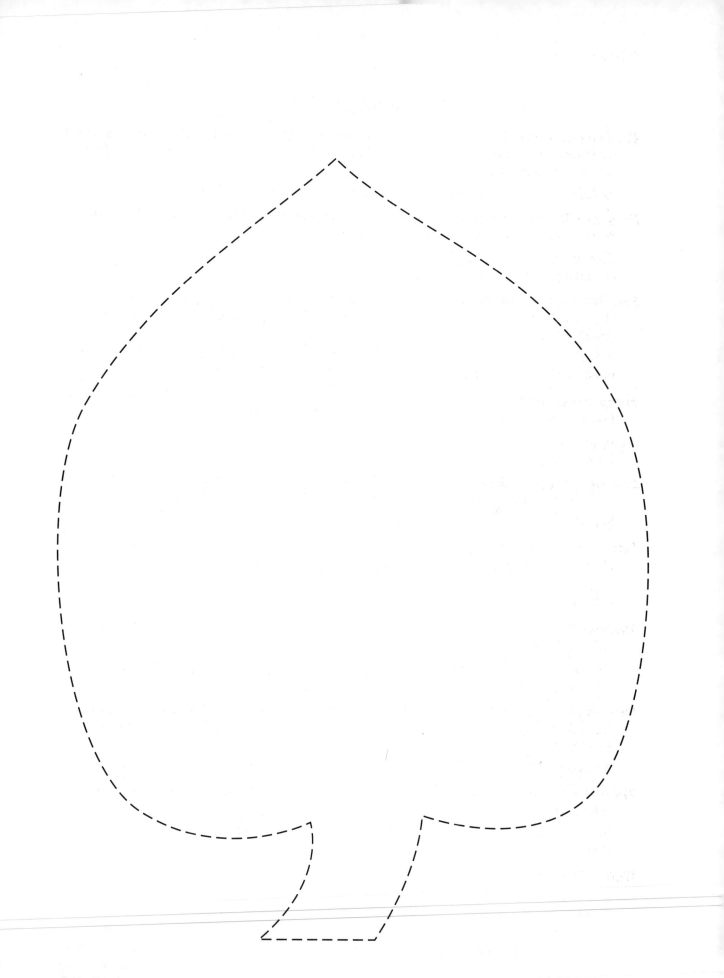

Lily Pad Pattern

Recommended Books

***The Frog Alphabet Book and Other Awesome Amphibians* by Jerry Pallotta, illustrated by Ralph Masiello** (Watertown, MA: Charlesbridge, 1990); full-color illustrations; Interest Level: K-3; Reading Level: 4.8.

Alphabet identifies, illustrates, and describes amphibians from A to Z.

***Frog and Toad Are Friends* written and illustrated by Arnold Lobel** (New York: Harper & Row, 1970); two-color illustrations; Interest Level: K-3; Reading Level: 2.4.

Contains five short stories about the gentle and humorous friendship between the two opposite personalities of a frog and a toad.

***Frog Went A-Courtin'* by John Langstaff, illustrated by Feodor Rojankovsky** (New York: Harcourt Brace Jovanovich, 1995/1983/1991); full-color illustrations; Interest Level: K-3; Reading Level: 2.7.

A frog courts a mouse and invites their animal friends to the wedding. Includes lyrics and music to this classic song.

***Jump, Frog, Jump* by Robert Kalan, illustrated by Byron Barton** (New York: Greenwillow Books, 1981); full-color illustrations; Interest Level: K-3; Reading Level: 2.1.

In this cumulative tale, a frog tries to catch a fly while, at the same time, eluding a fish, snake, turtle, and group of boys.

***Let's Go, Froggy!* by Jonathan London, illustrated by Frank Remiewicz** (New York: Viking, 1994); full-color illustrations; Interest Level: K-3; Reading Level: not listed.

Forgetful Froggy prepares for an outing with his mother and father.

***Little Frog's Song* by Alice Schertle, illustrated by Leonard Everett Fisher** (New York: HarperCollins, 1992); full-color illustrations; Interest Level: K-3; Reading Level: 4.7.

A little frog far from home enlists the help of a sheep, a dog, and finally a boy to return him to his pond.

***Max and Felix* by Larry Dane Brimmer, illustrated by Les Gray** (Honesdale, PA: Bell Books, 1993); full-color illustrations; Interest Level: K-3; Reading Level: not listed.

Two zany frog friends, Max and Felix, test their friendship as they skateboard, build a porch, tell a story, and go fishing together.

***Over in the Meadow* based on original version by Olive A. Wadsworth, illustrated by Ezra Jack Keats** (New York: Scholastic, 1971); full-color illustrations; Interest Level: K-3; Reading Level: 2.3.

A meadow is alive with the lyrical sights and sounds of the animals that live there.

***Tiddalick the Frog* by Susan Nunes, illustrated by Ju-Hong Chen** (New York: Atheneum, 1989); full-color illustrations; Interest Level: K-3; Reading Level: 2.3.

In this Australian Aboriginal tale, a tiny eel persuades an enormous frog named Tiddalick to give water to the earth.

***Walter Was a Frog* by Diane Redfield Massie** (New York: Simon and Schuster, 1970); two-color illustrations; Interest Level: K-3; Reading Level: 1.0.

Walter tries to be a bird and a fish until he realizes he is happiest as a frog.

Nonfiction Resources

***At the Frog Pond* by Tilde Michels, illustrated by Reinhard Michl, translated from German by Nina Ignatowicz** (Philadelphia: J.B. Lippincott, 1989); three-color illustrations; Interest Level: K-3; Reading Level: 3.7.

Poetic text and glistening illustrations describe animal life at a frog pond during spring and summer.

***The Frog* by Margaret Lane, illustrated by Grahame Corbett** (New York: Dial Press, 1981); full-color illustrations; Interest Level: K-3; Reading Level: 5.6.

Presents life cycle, habitat, and uses of frogs in the modern world.

***Frogs in Three Dimensions* by Jill Bailey, illustrated by Jerome Bruandet** (New York: Viking, 1992); full-color illustrations; Interest Level: K-3; Reading Level: not listed.

Pop-up, lift-the-flap, and pull-the-tab mechanical devices in the book, as well as the text, explain the habitat, feeding, movement, reproduction, and defense strategies of frogs.

***From Tadpole to Frog* by Wendy Pfeffer, illustrated by Holly Keller** (New York: Harper-Collins, 1994); full-color illustrations; Interest Level: K-3; Reading Level: 2.5.

Explains the life cycle of the frog.

***Lily Pad Pond*, text and photographs by Bianca Lavies** (New York: E.P. Dutton, 1989); full-color photographs; Interest Level: K-3; Reading Level: 3.0.

Large, colorful photographs and text capture the diversity of creatures at a lily pond.

Recipe: Swamp Juice

1 ripe banana, cut into chunks

1 cup orange juice, chilled

1 cup skim milk

2 ice cubes

6 drops green food coloring

1/4 teaspoon vanilla extract

optional: 1/4 cup white sugar

This recipe makes about three cups or three 8-ounce servings. Place all of the ingredients in an electric blender. Cover and blend on high speed until the mixture is smooth. If necessary, sweeten to taste with additional sugar. Serve.

Music Activity: "The Frog Song"

Cut out and color the three accompanying illustrations to illustrate the verses.

THE FROG SONG (Sung to the tune "Ain't It Great.")

Ain't it great to be frog eggs, Ti– ny specks in a

pond.   Ain't it great to be in a jel– ly glob,

Ain't it great to be frog eggs.

Verse 1: Ain't it great to be frog eggs,
Tiny specks in a pond.
Ain't it great to be in a jelly glob,
Ain't it great to be frog eggs.

During the entire verse, sing the verse curled up in a ball.

Verse 2: Ain't it great to be tadpoles,
Swimming free in a pond.
Ain't it great to be cute polliwogs,
Ain't it great to be tadpoles.

Sing this verse standing with arms at your sides, feet together, and moving your torso.

Verse 3: Ain't it great to be froggies,

Stand proudly looking as though you have hooked your thumbs through a pair of suspenders.

Ain't it great to have legs.

Slap your legs.

Ain't it great to eat big, juicy bugs,

Rub your stomach.

Ain't it great to be froggies.

Again, stand proudly with your thumbs seemingly hooked to a pair of suspenders.

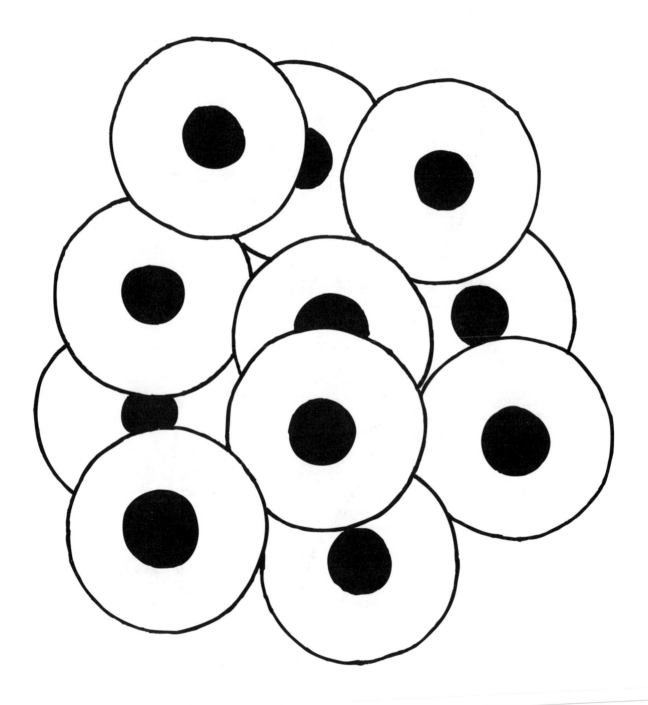

Frog Eggs

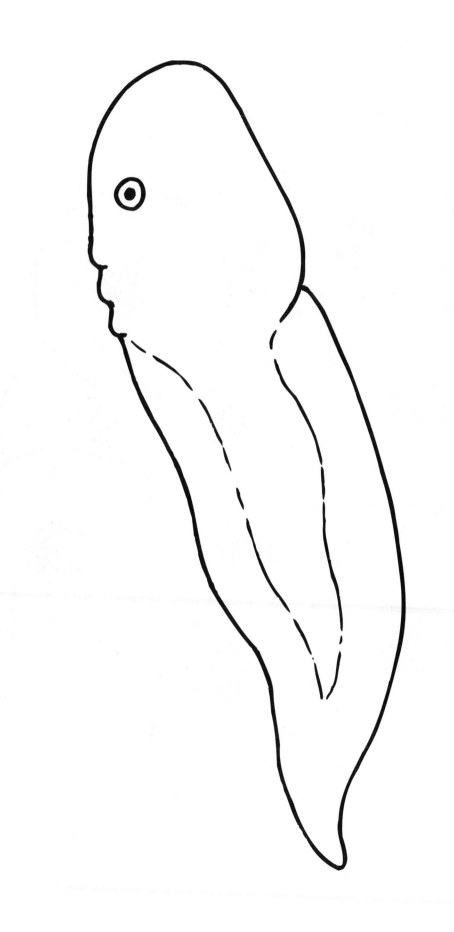

Tadpole

Frog

Art Activity: Frog Hats

Materials:

- blue 18-inch by 12-inch construction paper
- photocopies of the frog pattern
- crayons
- safety scissors
- glue
- cotton balls (two balls per student)
- mini-circle stickers (two stickers per child)
- large paper clips (one per child)

Preparation:

Make copies of the frog pattern so that each child gets a copy. Cut construction paper into strips measuring 2 inches by 18 inches. Form the strips into circles, joining the ends with a large paper clip. Each child should receive one circle.

Procedure:

Have students color and cut out the frogs along the dotted lines. Glue a cotton ball on each "x" and place a mini-circle on each cotton ball to serve as eyes. Tape the four legs to the top edge of the head band circle. Have the students wear the frog hats and adjust the head bands to fit their heads.

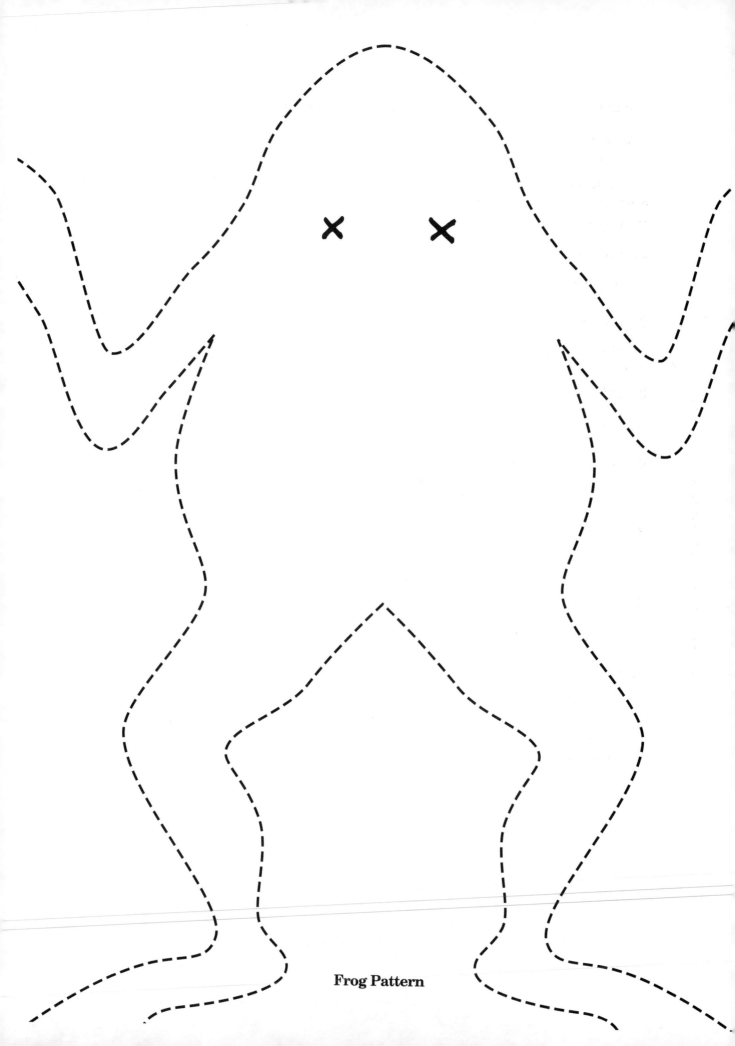

Frog Pattern

Name _____ Date _____

Classroom Teacher _____

Frogs Research Project: Use a reference source, such as an encyclopedia, that contains color photographs of a wide variety of frogs. Look at the pictures and answer these questions:

1. Do you see a frog with red coloring?   _____

   If so, what is the name of the frog? _____

2. Do you see a frog with orange coloring?   _____

   If so, what is the name of the frog? _____

3. Do you see a frog with yellow coloring?   _____

   If so, what is the name of the frog? _____

4. Do you see a frog with green coloring?   _____

   If so, what is the name of the frog? _____

5. Do you see a frog with blue coloring?   _____

   If so, what is the name of the frog? _____

6. Do you see a frog with brown coloring?   _____

   If so, what is the name of the frog? _____

7. Do you see a frog with black coloring?   _____

   If so, what is the name of the frog? _____

Write the name of the book where you found your information:

_____

What has 18 legs and catches flies?

A baseball team!

Gingerbread

Getting Ready to Teach the Letter G

Set the stage for this unit by placing a simmer pot—filled with water, cinnamon, cloves, and orange and lemon peels—in an area where students do not have access and cannot accidentally burn themselves. Turn on the simmer pot shortly before class begins. Wear an apron and display baking implements around the library.

Objectives for Gingerbread:

Each child will be able to:

1. Match the letter "G" with the word "gingerbread" and vice versa.
2. Summarize the read-aloud story in chronological order.
3. List the ingredients and procedure necessary to create gingerbread.

Introductory Activity: Baking Cookies

Before class begins, make or purchase enough gingerbread cookies and napkins for the entire class. When students come to class, tell them that although the last class had gingerbread cookies, we do not have enough ingredients to make cookies in this class and we therefore have to make imaginary cookies. Ask the children to take out their imaginary mixing bowls and wooden spoons. Next, ask the children how much of each ingredient (flour, sugar, eggs, etc.) we will need. As each child responds, pretend to add that ingredient to the mixture. Finally, pretend to shape the dough into cookies and put the cookies in the oven to bake. While the rest of the class goes to the story corner to read a story, one of the children quietly puts a napkin and cookie at each seat so that children can enjoy a cookie together after listening to the story.

Recommended Books

***Ben's Gingerbread Man* by Niki Daly** (New York: Viking Penguin, 1985); full-color illustrations; Interest Level: K-3; Reading Level: 1.5.

When Ben's mom accidentally sits on Ben's gingerbread man and breaks it, she makes Ben several more gingerbread men to replace the first one.

***The Cookie House* by Margaret Hillert, illustrated by Kinuko Craft** (New York: Modern Curriculum, 1978); full-color illustrations; Interest Level: K-3; Reading Level: 1.4.

This classic fairy tale recounts the story of two children who are lost in the woods and wander to a gingerbread house inhabited by a wicked witch.

***The Gingerbread Boy* by Paul Galdone** (New York: Seabury Press; 1975); full-color illustrations; Interest Level: K-3; Reading Level: 3.7.

Galdone recounts the story of the cookie that outfoxes everyone except a fox.

***The Gingerbread Doll* by Susan Tews, illustrated by Megan Lloyd** (New York: Clarion Books, 1993); full-color illustrations; Interest Level: K-3; Reading Level: 4.6.

A great-grandmother recalls her first doll, constructed of gingerbread, which her mother lovingly made her when the family was too poor to afford a porcelain doll.

***The Gingerbread Man* retold by Eric A. Kimmel, illustrated by Megan Lloyd** (New York: Holiday House, 1993); full-color illustrations; Interest Level: K-3; Reading Level: 2.1.

Large, colorful illustrations recount the classic story of a gingerbread boy who runs away and finally is devoured by a fox.

***The Gingerbread Man in Signed English* adapted by Michelle A. Herx** (New York: Kendall Green Publications, 1976); full-color illustrations; Interest Level: K-3; Reading Level: 2.1.

Contains illustrations of the classic gingerbread story plus a presentation of the story in Signed English.

***The Gingerbread Rabbit* by Jarrell Randell** (New York: HarperCollins, 1964/1992); black-and-white illustrations; Interest Level: K-3; Reading Level: 2.0.

A gingerbread rabbit, which Mother made as a treat for her daughter, escapes from the house, eludes a tricky fox, and befriends two kind rabbits. This book is relatively long and probably would require more than one sitting to read it to the class.

***Hansel and Gretel* by Eduard Jose, retold by Janet Richecky, illustrated by Agusti Asensio** (Elgin, IL: Child's World, 1988); full-color illustrations; Interest Level: K-3; Reading Level: 4.6.

This classic Grimm Brothers tale is the story of two children, abandoned by their father, who wander aimlessly in the woods until they discover a gingerbread house owned by a wicked witch.

***The Queen Who Couldn't Bake Gingerbread* by Dorothy Van Noerkom, illustrated by Paul Galdone** (New York: Alfred A. Knopf, 1975); full-color illustrations; Interest Level: K-3; Reading Level: 3.9.

A kind king seeks a woman who bakes gingerbread and finally marries a woman who doesn't bake. Slowly both spouses realize that kindness, wisdom, and love are the most important qualities in a spouse.

Nonfiction Resources

***The Cookie Cookbook* by John F. Carafoli, illustrated by John Craig** (New York: Follet Publishing Co., 1977); full-color illustrations; Interest Level: K-3; Reading Level: not listed.

Contains simple recipes and instructions for twelve types of cookies including gingerbread people.

***The International Cookie Jar Cookbook: Recipes from All Over the World* by Anita Borghese, illustrated by Yaroslava Mills** (New York: Charles Scribner's Sons, 1975); black-and-white illustrations; Interest and Reading Levels: not listed.

Presents recipes for cookies representing 67 countries with an introduction to each recipe.

***It's a Gingerbread House: Bake It, Build It, Eat It!* by Vera B. Williams** (New York: Greenwillow Books, 1978); full-color illustrations; Interest Level: K-3; Reading Level: 3.4.

This book contains instructions to bake and create a gingerbread house.

***KidsCooking: A Very Slightly Messy Manual* by the editors of Klutz Press, illustrated by Jim M'Guinness** (Palo Alto, CA: Klutz Press, 1987); full-color illustrations; Interest and Reading Levels: not listed.

Simple, imaginative, kid-pleasing recipes with clear, well-illustrated directions.

***My First Cookbook* by Rena Coyle, illustrated by Jerry Joyner** (New York: Workman Publishing, 1985); full-color and black-and-white illustrations; Interest Level: K-3; Reading Level: 4.5.

Bialosky the teddy bear hosts this colorful cookbook featuring kid-pleasing recipes. Check the recipes for gingerbread Christmas cards and gingerbread bear's hearts.

***Sugar* by Rhoda Nottridge, illustrated by John Yates** (Minneapolis: Carolrhoda Books, 1989); full-color illustrations; Interest Level: 3-6; Reading Level: 4.1.

Explains the origin, history, processing, and uses of sugar. Includes simple recipes.

Recipe: Ginger Spice Cookies

1 cup butter, softened to room temperature	1-1/2 teaspoons baking soda
1 cup brown sugar	1 teaspoon ginger
1 egg	1/2 teaspoon cloves
1/4 cup light molasses	1/2 teaspoon cinnamon
3 tablespoons maple syrup	1/2 teaspoon salt
2-1/2 cups all-purpose flour, sifted	3/4 cup white granulated sugar

This recipe makes about 3 dozen cookies. Preheat oven to 375 degrees. Cream shortening and brown sugar. Add egg, molasses, and maple syrup. Gently add flour, baking soda, ginger, cloves, cinnamon, and salt. Chill dough at least 2 hours. Form dough into 1-1/2-inch balls, roll in white sugar, and bake on a greased cookie sheet for 12 to 15 minutes.

Music Activity: "A Gingerbread Boy"

Refer to the accompanying finger plays on page 69.

A GINGERBREAD BOY (Sung to the tune "The Farmer in the Dell.")

Verse 2: First you add the flour,
The sugar and the spice.
We're going to make,
We're going to bake,
A gingerbread boy.

Verse 3: Then you stir and mix,
Then you mix and stir.
We're going to make,
We're going to bake,
A gingerbread boy.

Verse 4: Then you roll the dough,
And cut it carefully.
We're going to make,
We're going to bake,
A gingerbread boy.

Verse 5: Then you let it bake,
And then you take it out.
Oh, what a treat,
We're going to eat a gingerbread boy,
CRUNCH!

Verse 1

A gingerbread boy,
A gingerbread boy.

(Use fingers to draw the shape of a gingerbread boy in the air.)

We're going to make,
We're going to bake a gingerbread boy.

(Rub tummy.)

Verse 2

First you add the flour,
The sugar and the spice.

(Pretend to hold a bowl and pour ingredients into the bowl.)

We're going to make,
we're going to bake a gingerbread boy.

(Rub tummy.)

Verse 3

Then you stir and mix,
Then you mix and stir.

(Pretend to stir ingredients in imaginary bowl.)

We're going to make,
We're going to bake a gingerbread boy.

(Rub tummy.)

Verse 4

Then you roll the dough
And cut it carefully.

(Pretend to roll dough with a rolling pin and cut out shapes with a cookie cutter.)

We're going to make,
We're going to bake a gingerbread boy.

(Rub tummy.)

Verse 5

Then you let it bake,
And then you take it out.

(Pretend to open oven door and insert cookie sheet, then open oven door and remove cookie sheet.)

Oh, what a treat,
We're going to eat a gingerbread boy.

(Rub tummy.)

CRUNCH!

(Open mouth and pretend to eat cookie.)

Art Activity: Gingerbread Man

Materials:

- pen
- safety scissors
- brown construction paper (one piece per student)
- gingerbread man pattern
- colored chalk
- cardboard

Preparation:

Trace the gingerbread man pattern onto a piece of cardboard. Using the cardboard as a template, trace the gingerbread shape onto each piece of brown construction paper.

Procedure:

Have students use colored chalk to decorate the gingerbread man and cut him out.

Gingerbread Man Pattern

Name _____ Date _____

Classroom Teacher _____

Gingerbread Research Project: Look up "gingerbread" in a cookbook. List the ingredients in gingerbread on the lines below.

_____

_____

_____

_____

_____

_____

_____

_____

Write the title of the book where you found your information:

_____

_____

Home

Getting Ready to Teach the Letter H

Dress for this unit by wearing a paint hat, paint-spattered overalls, work boots, and a tool belt containing a hammer, screwdriver, and other woodworking tools. Also, if you complete the introductory activity, carry a small bucket filled with water, a wide paintbrush, or a mini paint roller.

Objectives for Home:

Each child will be able to:

1. Match the letter "H" with the word "home" and vice versa.

2. Summarize the read-aloud story in chronological order.

3. Describe the physical characteristics of a home.

Introductory Activity: Home Drawing Story

The story below can be drawn with chalk on a chalkboard. For added fun, though, it can be completed by "painting" the chalkboard with water, using a wide paintbrush or mini roller, in lieu of chalk.

I'm building something. I'd like to tell you and show you what I am building. Can you guess what it is?

The thing I am drawing has many windows. I'm going to draw a window here.

This thing also has water pipes. I need to dig a v-shaped ditch . . .

. . . that runs from here to there.

The thing I am building also has stairs. I'm building three stairs here . . .

OME

. . . and a railing on the side.

OME

Finally, I'm building not one, but two driveways . . .

I IOME

. . . with a sidewalk between them. Who can tell me what I'm building?

HOME

Recommended Books

***Building a House* by Bryon Barton** (New York: Mulberry Books, 1981); full-color illustrations; Interest Level: K-3; Reading Level: 1.4.

Simple text and illustrations chronicle a house being built.

***Flora's Magic House* written and illustrated by Binette Schroeder** (New York: North-South Books, 1969); full-color illustrations; Interest Level: K-3; Reading Level: 4.2.

Flora the doll and her friends are carried away by her magic house as they seek new adventures.

***The Hidden House* by Martin Waddell and Angela Barrett** (New York: Putnam & Grosset Group, 1990); full-color illustrations; Interest Level: K-3; Reading Level: 4.0.

Three wooden dolls, left in a deserted house, are discovered and cared for by a family that restores the house to its original beauty.

***The House on Maple Street* by Bonnie Pryon, illustrated by Beth Peck** (New York: William Morrow and Co., 1987); full-color illustrations; Interest Level: K-3; Reading Level: 4.0.

A young girl digs up a china cup and arrow head from her yard and imagines the origin of these tiny treasures.

***The House That Jack Built* by Rodney Peppe** (New York: Delacorte Press, 1970); full-color illustrations; Interest Level: K-3; Reading Level: 2.0.

Lively collage illustrates the classic cumulative story of Jack and his house.

***In a People House* by Theodore LeSieg (Dr. Seuss), illustrated by Roy McKie** (New York: Random House, 1972); full-color illustrations; Interest Level: K-3; Reading Level: 2.3.

In this rollicking rhyming story, a mouse introduces a bird to the common objects found in a "people house."

***On Grandma's Roof* by Erica Silverman, illustrated by Deborah Kogan Ray** (New York: Macmillan, 1990); full-color illustrations; Interest Level: K-3; Reading Level: 2.0.

A young child and her grandmother hang laundry from the roof of a city apartment and enjoy each other's company.

***Our House on the Hill* by Philippe Dupasquier** (New York: Viking Kestrel, 1987); full-color illustrations; Interest Level: K-3; Reading Level: 2.0.

Wordless picture book shows the inside and outside activities of a family that lives in a house on the hill.

***Victoria House* by Janice Shefelman, illustrated by Tom Shefelman** (New York: Harcourt Brace Jovanovich, 1988); full-color illustrations; Interest Level: K-3; Reading Level: 3.6.

A family moves a Victorian house from the country to the city, restores it, and moves in.

***Village of Round and Square Houses* by Ann Grifalconi** (Boston: Little, Brown and Company, 1986); full-color illustrations; Interest Level: K-3; Reading Level: 3.8.

A grandmother from West Africa relates the legend that led to the custom of women living in round houses and men living in square ones.

Nonfiction Resources

***How a House Is Built* by Gail Gibbons** (New York: Holiday House, 1990); full-color illustrations; Interest Level: K-3; Reading Level: 3.0.

The author explains, through text and illustrations, how a traditional house is built, step-by-step.

***I Can Be a Carpenter* by Dee Lillegard** (Chicago: Children's Press, 1986); full-color illustrations and photographs; Interest Level: K-3; Reading Level: 3.3.

Presents the tools and responsibilities of carpenters as well as the structures they help to build.

***Other People, Other Homes!* by Barry Milton, pictures by John Lobben** (New York: Gareth Stevens Publishing, 1985); full-color illustrations; Interest Level: K-3; Reading Level: 4.1.

Explores, through text and illustrations, the homes and recreational activities of 20 ethnic groups and nationalities throughout the world.

***Pete's House* by Harriet Langsam Sobol, photographs by Patricia Agre** (New York: Macmillan, 1978); black-and-white photographs; Interest Level: 3-6; Reading Level: 4.3.

Illustrations and text tell the story of a young boy as he watches his house being built.

***This Is My House* written and illustrated by Arthur Dorros** (New York: Scholastic, 1992); full-color illustrations; Interest Level: K-3; Reading Level: 3.1.

Presents typical houses throughout the world as well as the pronunciation and spelling of "This is my house" in various languages.

Recipe: Graham Cracker Houses

12 graham crackers

1 batch of royal icing (see recipe below)

12 tablespoons regular cake frosting

assorted colored cereals, candies, miniature marshmallows, pretzel sticks, etc.

This recipe makes four houses. Before class begins, use a knife to score the graham crackers before breaking them into 24 equal squares. Use the graham crackers to create four walls in each of four structures, using the royal icing squeezed from a pastry bag, to join the sides. When the structure is firm, use two additional graham cracker squares and royal icing to create a roof for each structure. When firm, give one graham cracker house, as well as an assortment of decorations and 3 tablespoons cake frosting, to each student. Have each student decorate his or her house with the decorations, using the frosting to glue on the decorations.

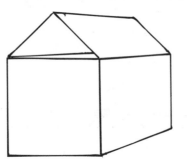

Royal icing is not regular cake or cookie icing. It can be made by combining 1-1/3 cups confectioner's sugar, 1 tablespoon meringue powder (available at specialty cake decorating stores), and 1-1/2 tablespoons warm water. Keep the frosting in a pastry bag.

Music Activity: "My Cozy Home"

Refer to the additional verses and accompanying finger plays on pages 78 and 79.

MY COZY HOME (Sung to the tune "The Wheels on the Bus.")

Verse 2:   My cozy home has clear, glass windows,
Clear, glass windows,
Clear, glass windows.
My cozy home has clear glass windows,
So I can see outside.

Verse 3:   My cozy home has a roof overhead,
Roof overhead,
Roof overhead.
My cozy home has a roof overhead,
To shelter me from the storms.

Verse 4:   My cozy home has people who love me,
People who love me,
People who love me.
My cozy home has people who love me,
And I love them, too.

Finger Plays:

Verse 1

Verse 2

Verse 3

Verse 4: Lines 1-4   Verse 4: Line 5

ozy home has strong, sturdy walls,
ng, sturdy walls,
Strong, sturdy walls.
My cozy home has strong, sturdy walls,
To keep me safe and sound.

(Move hands in the air as if feeling a wall.)

Verse 2 My cozy home has clear, glass windows
Clear, glass windows,
Clear, glass windows.
My cozy home has clear, glass windows,
So I can see outside.

(Moving hands in a circular motion, pretend to wash windows.)

(Cup hands to eyes as if peering through a window.)

Verse 3 My cozy home has a roof overhead,
A roof overhead,
A roof overhead.
My cozy home has a roof overhead,
To shelter me from the storms.

(Use hand to make a peak over head.)

(Move fingers from head to toe to represent rain.)

Verse 4 My cozy home has people who love me,
People who love me,
People who love me.
My cozy home has people who love me,
And I love them too.

(Clasp hands across body as if giving oneself a hug.)

(Point to eye, cross hands over heart, then hold arms wide as if embracing everyone.)

Art Activity: Home Bank

Materials:

- photocopies of the two house patterns* (both patterns for each child)
- empty, clean half-pint milk cartons (one carton per child)
- scissors
- glue
- crayons
- stapler and staples

Procedure:

Have students cut out the rectangular portion of the milk carton that makes the spout. This will be the slot where the children will drop their coins. Next, have students color and cut out the house patterns and glue them to the milk cartons. Staple the roof to the top of the carton.

*Half-pint milk containers usually measure 2-3/4" W x 2-3/4" D x 3-1/2" H **or** 2-1/4" W x 2-1/4" D x 4-1/4" H. The house patterns given here accommodate both sizes.

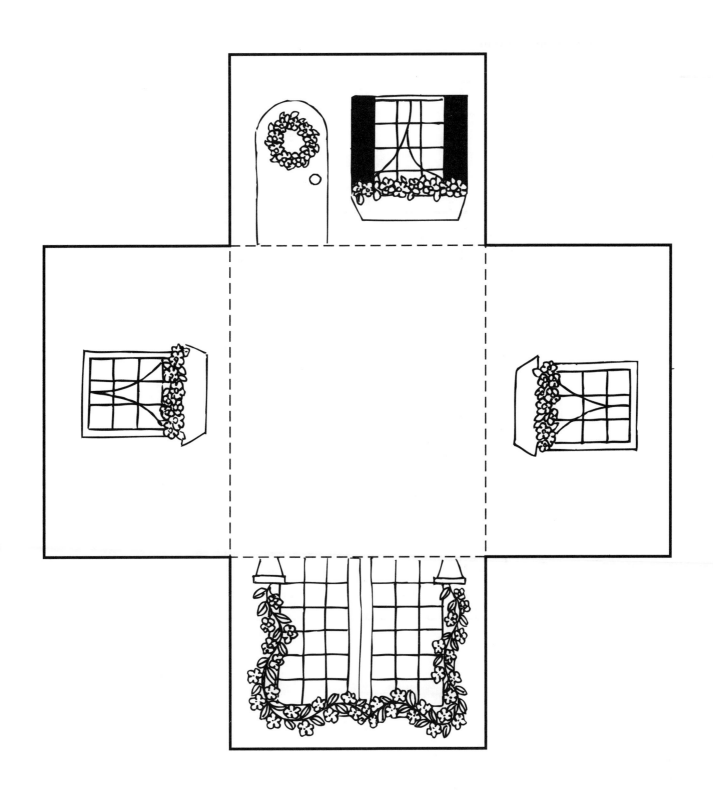

For milk cartons measuring
2-3/4" wide x 2-3/4" deep x 3-1/2" high

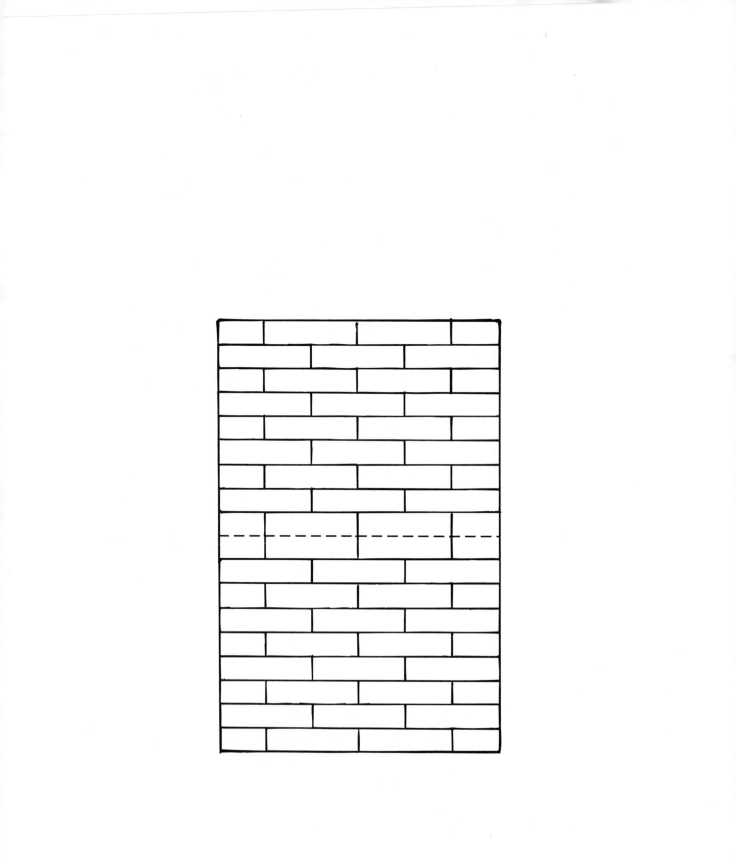

Roof for milk carton measuring 2-3/4" wide x 2-3/4" deep x 3-1/2" high

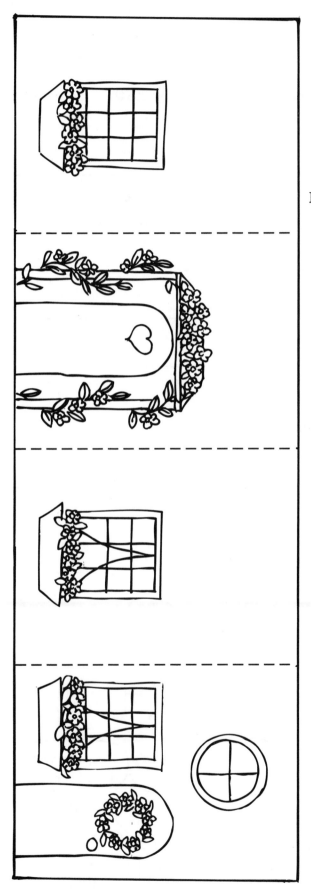

House

**For milk carton measuring 2-1/4"
wide x 2-1/4" deep x 4-1/4" high**

Roof

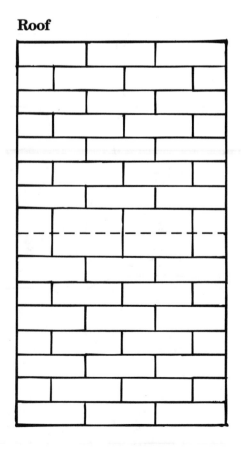

Name _____ Date _____

Classroom Teacher _____

Home Research Project: Look up "home" in a thesaurus. Write the synonyms for "home" on the lines below.

_____

_____

_____

_____

_____

Write the title of the book where you found your information:

_____

Insects

Getting Ready to Teach the Letter I

Before class begins, dress in a black sweat suit and sunglasses and wear a plastic headband to which you have attached pipe cleaners twisted to resemble antennae. Gather a yard of white nylon netting (available at many fabric stores) in the middle and pin it to the back of your sweat shirt to resemble wings and attach two long, black fabric strips to resemble additional legs. When children enter the library, ask them to guess what animal you are. When they guess that you are an insect, ask them to tell you the clues they need to determine that you are an insect. Those clues might include the following:

1. All insects have six legs.
2. All insects have a head, thorax, and abdomen.
3. Most insects have wings and antenna.
4. Most adult insects have compound eyes.

Here are additional interesting facts about insects you may want to share with your students:

1. The skeleton of an insect is on the outside of its body.
2. Many insects taste with their feet and smell with their antenna.
3. Scientists have discovered 800,000 kinds of insects.
4. Insects live in most parts of the world.
5. The largest insect is the Atlas moth which has a wing span of ten inches. One of the smallest insects is the fairy fly which is one-hundredth of an inch long.
6. Scientists estimate that there may be as many as 30 million species of insects.
7. The oldest known insect lived 420 million years ago.
8. The longest insect was a walking stick from Africa that measured 15-3/4 inches.

Objectives for Insects:

Each child will be able to:

1. Match the letter "I" with the word "insect" and vice versa.
2. Summarize the read-aloud story in chronological order.
3. List the common physical characteristics of all insects and name several species of insects.

Introductory Activity: Insect Riddles

1. Photocopy the "buggy" riddles and six copies each of the insect wings and insect body patterns.
2. Color the insect wings and body and cut them out. Cut out the insect riddles and answers.
3. Glue an insect riddle on one wing and the corresponding answer on the insect body.

4. Use a brad to attach the insect wings to the body.

5. Place the wings together, show the insect to the children, and ask them the insect riddle. When they answer the riddle correctly, spread the wings to reveal the correct answer.

6. HINT: Save the insects to create a bulletin board.

BUGGY RIDDLES

Which insect carries its own flashlight?	a firefly
Which insect likes to sleep the most?	a bedbug
Which insect goes to church?	a praying mantis
Which insect only dates gentlemen bugs?	a ladybug
Which insect wears a saddle and bridle?	a horsefly
Which insect can be baked, mashed, or french fried?	a potato bug

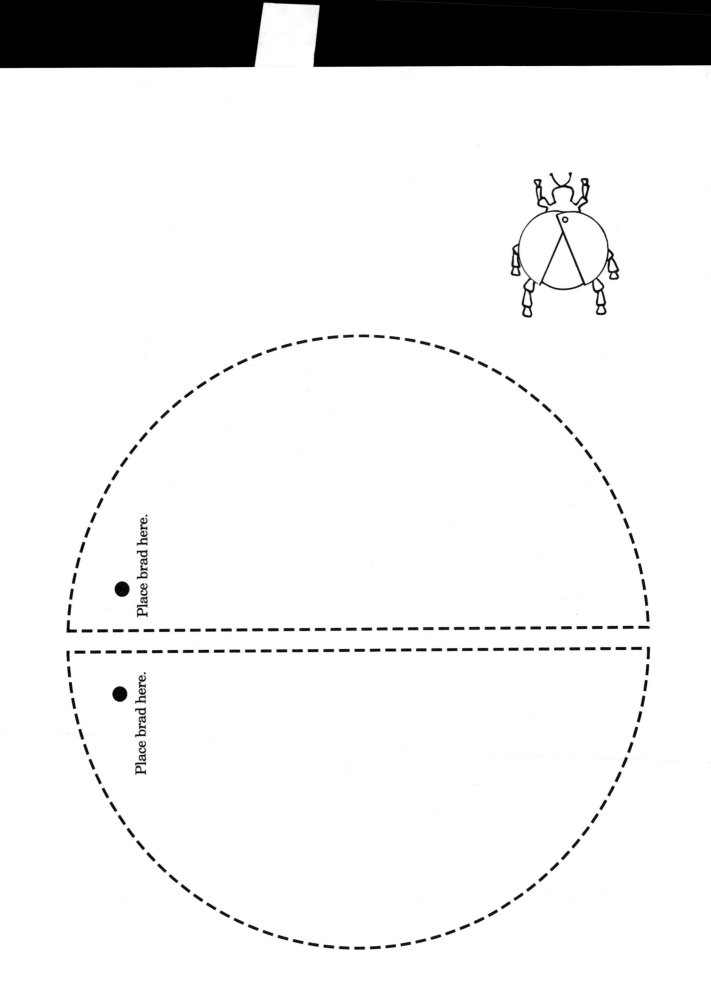

Place brad here.

Place brad here.

Insect Wing Patterns

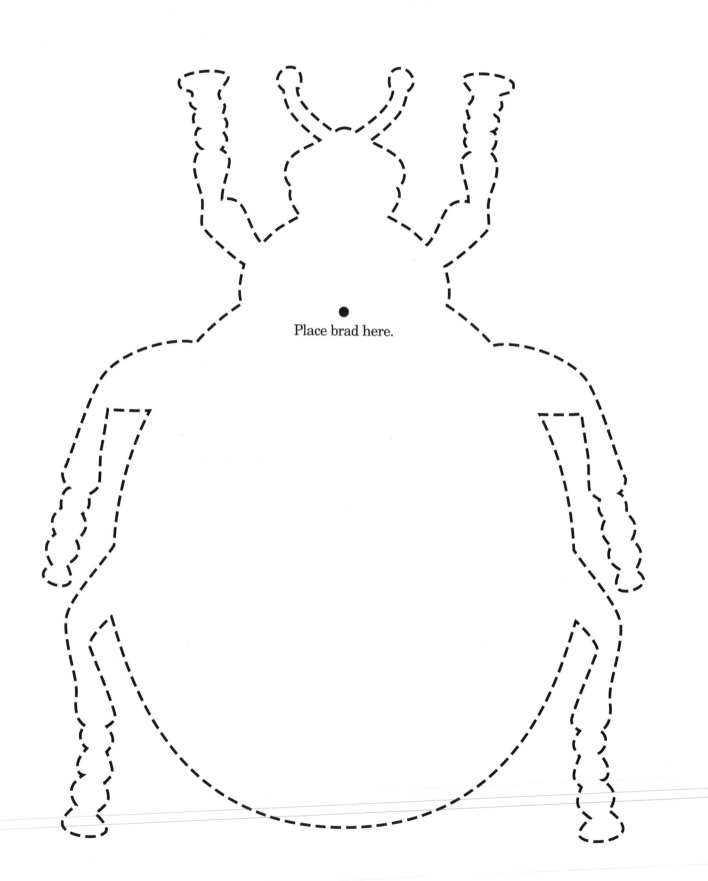

Place brad here.

Insect Body Pattern

Recommended Books

***Antics: An Alphabet Anthology* by Cathi Hepworth** (New York: G.P. Putnam's Sons, 1992); full-color illustrations; Interest Level: 3-6; Reading Level: 5.5.

This ABC book presents humorous ants in fantastical costumes and situations to demonstrate a word representing each letter of the alphabet.

***Bug City* written and illustrated by Dahlov Ipcar** (New York: Holiday House, 1975); full-color illustrations; Interest Level: K-3; Reading Level: 3.5.

Using puns and jokes, the author describes the insect citizens of Bug City.

***Bugs* by Patricia and Frederick McKissack, illustrated by Clovis Martin** (Chicago: Children's Press, 1988); full-color illustrations; Interest Level: K-3; Reading Level: 1.4.

Counting book introduces the numerals one through five.

***Fireflies* written and illustrated by Julie Brinkloe** (New York: Macmillan, 1985); two-color illustrations; Interest and Reading Levels: not listed.

A young child catches fireflies on a summer night and realizes that he should let them go.

***A Fly Went By* by Mike McClintock, illustrated by Fritz Siebel** (New York: Random House, 1958); Interest Level: K-3; Reading Level: 2.5.

Cumulative rhyming tale about a fly running away from a frog which is running away from a cat, etc.

***I Know an Old Lady* by Rose Bonne, illustrated by William Stobbs** (New York: Scholastic, 1994); full-color illustrations; Interest Level: K-3; Reading Level: 1.7.

Classic song/story about an old woman who swallows a fly, a spider, a bird, a cat, a dog, a goat, a cow, and finally a horse. She's dead, of course.

***The Icky Bug Counting Book* by Jerry Pallotta, illustrated by Ralph Masiello** (Watertown, MA: Charlesbridge, 1992); full-color illustrations; Interest Level: K-3; Reading Level: 4.8.

Names, illustrates, and identifies common and exotic insects from 1 to 10.

***Nicholas Cricket* by Joyce Manner, illustrated by William Joyce** (New York: Harper & Row, 1989); full-color illustrations; Interested Level: K-3; Reading Level: 1.7.

Nickolas Cricket and his Bug-a-Wug Cricket Band entertain the forest animals at night.

***Old Black Fly* by Jim Aylesworth, illustrated by Stephen Gammell** (New York: Holt, 1992); full-color illustrations; Interest Level: K-3; Reading Level: 1.9.

The author introduces the ABC's through a lilting poem about the antics of an old black fly.

***Two Bad Ants* by Chris Van Allsburg** (Boston: Houghton Mifflin, 1988); full-color illustrations; Interest Level: K-3; Reading Level: 3.9.

Two ants, searching for sugar crystals for the queen ant, leave the colony and journey into the dangerous world of man.

Nonfiction Resources

***Ant Cities* written and illustrated by Arthur Dorros** (New York: HarperCollins, 1987); full-color illustrations; Interest Level: K-3; Reading Level: 2.6.

Describes various types of ants, ant hills, growth cycles, and ant communities.

Bugs **by Nancy Winslow Parker and Joan Richards Wright, illustrated by Nancy Winslow Parker** (New York: Greenwillow Books, 1987); full-color illustrations; Interest Level: K-3; Reading Level: 3.3.

Children can read this book on two levels, basic and advanced, to learn about a variety of insects.

The Insect Almanac: A Year-Round Activity Guide **by Monica Russo, photographs by Kevin Byron** (New York: Sterling Publishing Co., 1991); black-and-white and color photographs and illustrations; Interest Level: young adult; Reading Level: not listed.

Contains a plethora of information about insects as well as a variety of activities to encourage budding entomologists.

Insect Coloring Book **by Jan Slovak** (New York: Dover Publications, 1994); black-line drawings; Interest and Reading Levels: not listed.

Presents 40 insects in their natural habitats.

What Is an Insect? **by Jennifer Day, illustrated by Dorothea Barlowe** (Racine, WI: Golden Press, 1976); full-color illustrations; Interest Level: K-3; Reading Level: not listed.

Contains bright illustrations and brief descriptions about insect families.

Recipe: Bug Crackers

1 box round crackers

1 box softened cream cheese or peanut butter

1 bag thin stick pretzels

1 box raisins

Spread cream cheese or peanut butter on a cracker. Place six pretzels on the cream cheese or peanut butter to resemble insect legs. Place another cracker over the buttered cracker. Use cream cheese or peanut butter to "glue" raisin eyes to the head of the insect.

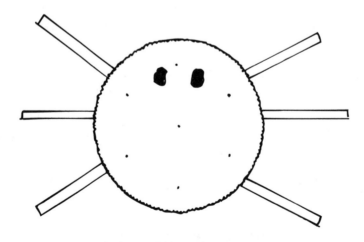

Music Activity: "Insect Song"

This is a jigsaw song. First, sing the song without motions. The second time, do not sing the word "abdomen"; instead, place your hand on your abdomen. The third time, repeat the abdomen motion, delete the word "thorax" and instead put your hand on your chest. The fourth time, repeat the motions for abdomen and thorax, delete the word "head" and instead put your hand on your head. The fifth time, repeat the motions for abdomen, thorax and head, delete the word "stinger," and pretend to pinch your arm.

THE INSECT SONG (Sung to the tune of "John Brown's Body.")

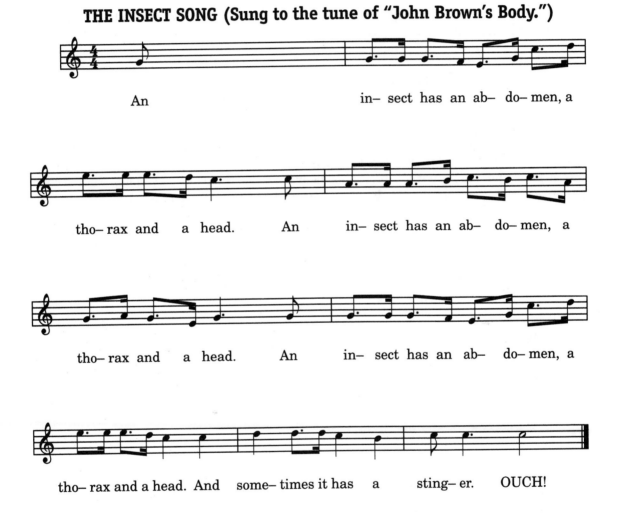

An ... in– sect has an ab– do– men, a

tho– rax and a head. An in– sect has an ab– do– men, a

tho– rax and a head. An in– sect has an ab– do– men, a

tho– rax and a head. And some– times it has a sting– er. OUCH!

Art Activity: Butterfly Pencil Topper

Materials:

- photocopies of the butterfly pattern
- crayons
- safety scissors
- paper punch
- sharpened pencils (one pencil per child)
- *optional:* 1/4-inch (3 mm) wiggle eyes and pencil topper erasers, which can be purchased in bulk from Holcomb's Educational Materials, 800-362-4445

Preparation:

Photocopy the butterfly pattern and cut the photocopies into quarters so that each child will receive one butterfly.

Directions:

Have students color and cut out their butterfly along the dotted line. Use a paper punch to cut two holes, where indicated, on the butterfly's body. Carefully thread the sharpened pencil through the two holes so that the butterfly is positioned near the top of the pencil. (*Optional:* Place a pencil topper eraser over the top of the pencil and glue two wiggle eyes on the eraser.)

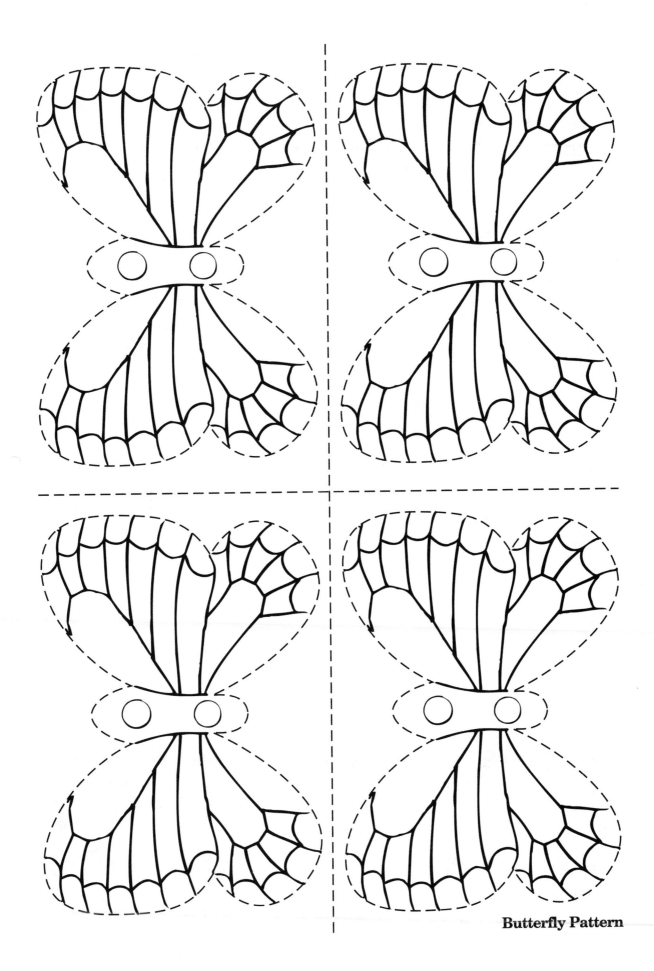

Butterfly Pattern

Name _____ Date _____

Classroom Teacher _____

Insects Research Project: Look up "insect" in an encyclopedia or other reference source. Identify each of the insects below and write the names on the lines just below the insects.

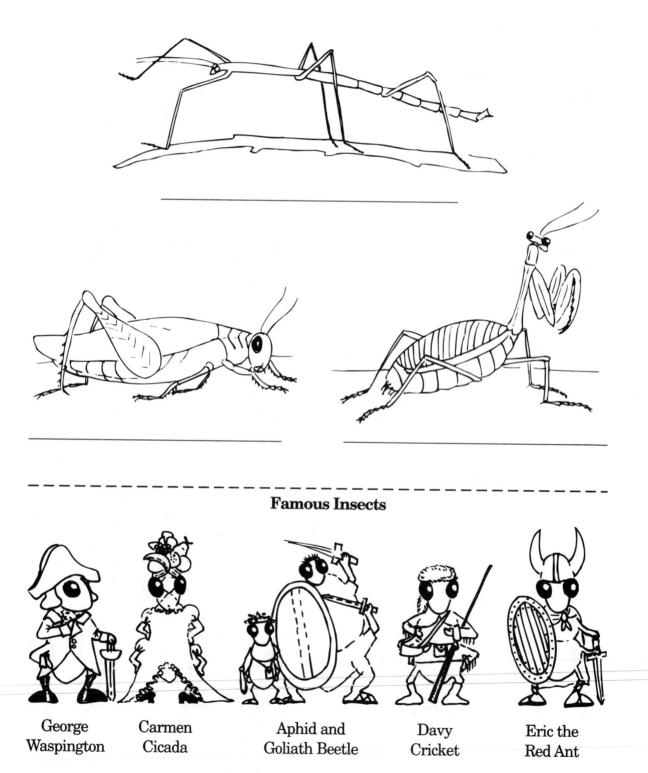

_____

_____   _____

Famous Insects

George
Waspington

Carmen
Cicada

Aphid and
Goliath Beetle

Davy
Cricket

Eric the
Red Ant

Jam and Jelly

Getting Ready to Teach the Letter J

Jams and jellies come in an amazing variety of colors and flavors. Display a variety of jars, coupled with a selection of related books, to make a colorful and attractive display.

Objectives for Jam and Jelly:

Each child will be able to:

1. Match the letter "J" with the words "jam" and "jelly" and vice versa.
2. Summarize the read-aloud story in chronological order.
3. Name the ingredients in jams and jellies and list several varieties of jams and jellies.

Introductory Activity: Jam and Jelly Taste Test

Materials:

- paper plates
- loaves of bread
- plastic knives
- an assortment of four jams and/or jellies
- *optional:* bite-size cookie cutters (available from Wilton Industries, 708-963-7100)

Procedure:

Distribute a paper plate, plastic knife, and slice of bread to each student. Have the children cut the slice of bread into four equal parts. (For added fun, have children use bite-size cookie cutters to cut out four shapes.) Distribute a teaspoon of each different jam or jelly to each student. Have the students spread the jam or jelly on their bread and sample each flavor. The class may want to construct a graph demonstrating the relative popularity of each jam or jelly.

Recommended Books

***Bread and Jam for Frances* by Russell Hoban, illustrated by Lillian Hoban** (New York: Harper & Row, 1964); black-and-white illustrations; Interest Level: K-3; Reading Level: 2.1.

Frances hardly touches her food because she prefers bread and jam. However, when her mother feeds her nothing but bread and jam, Frances changes her mind.

***The Giant Jam Sandwich* written and illustrated by John Vernon Lord, verses by Janet Burroway** (Boston: Houghton Mifflin, 1972); full-color illustrations; Interest Level: K-3; Reading Level: 3.4.

The villagers of Itching Down make a giant strawberry jam sandwich to capture a marauding hoard of wasps.

***Jamberry* written and illustrated by Bruce Degen** (New York: Harper & Row Scholastic, 1983); full-color illustrations; Interest Level: K-3; Reading Level: 2.5.

In this rhyme, a boy and a bear search the world for more and more delicious berries.

***Lionel and His Friends* by Stephen Krensky, pictures by Susanna Natti** (New York: Dial, 1996); full-color illustrations; Interest Level: K-3; Reading Level: 1.9.

The second chapter of this four-chapter book contains a story about Lionel and his friends in the school cafeteria. Lionel finds he does not want to eat his peanut butter and jelly sandwich and consequently trades his sandwich for his friend's tuna fish sandwich.

***The Lunch Box Surprise* by Grace Maccarone, illustrated by Betsy Lewin** (New York: Scholastic, 1995); full-color illustrations; Interest Level: K-3; Reading Level: not listed.

Sam looks in his lunch box and finds his mother forgot to pack his lunch. HIs friends share their lunch with him.

***Mother Raspberry* by Maurice Careme, pictures by Marie Wabbes** (New York: Thomas Y. Crowell Co., 1969); full-color illustrations; Interest Level: K-3; Reading Level: not listed.

The children in the village help Mother Raspberry in the summer and worry about Crooked Tail, a wolf, menacing the kind lady in the winter. Their fears are allayed, however, when they find that Mother Raspberry has befriended Crooked Tail and the other forest creatures.

***Mr. Putter and Tabby Pick the Pears* by Cynthia Rylant, illustrated by Arthur Howard** (New York: Harcourt Brace Jovanovich, 1995); full-color illustrations; Interest Level: K-3; Reading Level: 2.2.

An older gentleman, Mr. Putter, and his cat, Tabby, devise a way to pick pears to make pear jelly.

***Peanut Butter and Jelly: A Play Rhyme* by Nadine Bernard Westcott** (New York: Dutton Children's Book, 1987); full-color illustrations; Interest Level: K-3; Reading Level: 1.7.

Humorous, lyrical story about making and eating a peanut butter and jelly sandwich.

***Purple Delicious Blackberry Jam* by Lisa Westberg, illustrated by Barbara McGregor** (New York: Arcade Publishing, 1992); full-color illustrations; Interest Level: K-3; Reading Level: 2.4.

Reluctant Grandma is convinced by Freddy and Muff to make blackberry jam.

***Yellow Butter, Purple Jelly, Red Jam, Black Bread* by Mary Ann Hoberman, illustrated by Chaya Burstein** (New York: Viking Press, 1981); brown-tone illustrations; Interest Level: K-3; Reading Level: 3.5.

A collection of gently humorous poems for children including "Yellow Butter," a poem about jelly and jam.

Nonfiction Resources

***Bread, Bread, Bread* by Ann Morris, photographs by Ken Heyman** (New York: Lothrop, Lee & Shepard, 1989); full-color illustrations; Interest Level: K-3; Reading Level: 1.5.

Shows bread, in all of its forms, being prepared and eaten throughout the world.

***From Fruit to Jam* by Ali Mitgutsch** (Minneapolis: Carolrhoda Books, 1981); full-color illustrations; Interest Level: K-3; Reading Level: 3.7.

Explains how fresh fruits are transformed into jam.

***Making Bread* by Ruth Thomson, photographs by Chris Fairdough** (New York: Franklin Watts, 1987); full-color photographs; Interest Level: 3-6; Reading Level: 4.3.

Presents a tour of a bakery as bread is being prepared and baked.

***Sandwichery: Recipes, Riddles & Funny Facts About Food* by Patricia and Talivaldis Stubis** (New York: Parents Magazine Press, 1975); black-and-white and color illustrations; Interest Level and Reading Level: not listed.

Presents simple recipes, interesting historical facts, and humorous jokes about sandwiches.

A *Spoonful of Sugar* by Angela and Derek Lucas (New York: Bookwright Press, 1983); full-color illustrations; Interest Level: 3-6; Reading Level: 3.6.

Traces sugar from the sugarcane and beet farms to the processing plant to the grocery store to the kitchen. In addition, the book explains sugar's use and history.

Recipe: Jamsicles

3 tablespoons strawberry jam

16 ounces plain yogurt

10 ounces sliced strawberries with sugar

This recipe makes 12 jamsicles. Combine the above ingredients. Line cupcake tins with paper bake cups and pour the yogurt mixture into each one. Insert a popsicle stick into each cup and freeze.

Music Activity: "Musical Jam"

A jam not only can be found in the kitchen pantry. A jam is also a musical term in which the musicians improvise, or make up, the music as they are performing.

You will need an audio recording with a strong, steady beat for this activity. I recommend the theme song from the movie *Space Jam*. The audio recording is available from Atlantic Recording Corp., 75 Rockefeller Plaza, New York, New York 10019.

The objective of this activity is to play a recording and have the students join, one at a time, in the rhythm. Students can use their bodies and clap hands, snap fingers, stomp feet, etc. It is more fun, however, to use improvised or commercially prepared instruments. (Gamble Music Company, 312 South Wabash Avenue, Chicago, Illinois 60604 [1-800-621-4290], sells sets of rhythm instruments especially for young children.) Improvised instruments might include the following:

- sand blocks, which can be rubbed together rhythmically
- jingle bells, which are available at fabric and craft stores, can be strung onto paint stirring sticks
- 12-inch lengths of metal chains, when passed from hand to hand, make a rhythmic clinking sound
- 2 paint stirring sticks, hit together, make slap sticks
- covered metal cans or plastic containers, filled with small amounts of dried beans or popcorn kernels, can be shaken rhythmically

Have students sit in a circle, facing inward. Give each student a rhythm instrument. Turn on the music and, pointing to each student one-at-a-time, have the students keep the beat to the song.

Art Activity: Sniff-and-Color Bookmarks

Materials:

- extracts (see explanation below)
- photocopies of the jam/jelly pattern
- cotton swabs
- crayons
- safety scissors

Preparation:

Purchase several extracts at the herb/spice section of the grocery store. Some of the best selections include mint, orange, cherry, and strawberry extracts. Photocopy the jam/jelly patterns, one page per student. Shortly before class beings, use a cotton swab to rub a drop or two of each extract on one of the four jam/jelly pictures so that each slice of bread contains a different fragrance.

Procedure:

Have children color and cut out each jam/jelly picture and guess the extract flavor on each slice of bread. The completed pictures may be used as fragrant bookmarks.

Jam/Jelly Patterns

Name _____ Date _____

Classroom Teacher _____

Jam and Jelly Research Project: Look at the label on a jar of jam or jelly. Write the ingredients on the lines below.

Kings and Knights

Getting Ready to Teach the Letter K

Create a medieval atmosphere in the library/classroom by hanging simple construction paper coats of arms and playing theme-based music; I recommend the soundtracks from the motion pictures *First Knight* (available from Sony Music) or *Braveheart* (available from Decca Record Company). When children come to the library, choose one child to serve as king and have him (or her) sit in a chair that has been draped with gold lamé fabric. The king also can wear a crown and carry a scepter. The chairs and tables can be arranged to resemble a great hall. For those who are truly ambitious, create a castle by painting an empty refrigerator box gray and, using a wide-tipped permanent marker, create the illusion of stone walls.

In addition to the activities above, students can play several theme-related educational games using one or two identical decks of playing cards containing kings, queens, and jacks. First, punch a hole at the top of each card and string a length of yarn through each card to create card necklaces. Here are some game ideas:

1. Hand each child a card and give the class a specified length of time in which to line up in numerical order according to their card number.

2. Use two decks of cards to give identical cards to pairs of children. When you say "go," children are to find their "twin," join hands with the twin, and sit on the floor.

Objectives for Kings and Knights:

Each child will be able to:

1. Match the letter "K" with the words "king" and "knight," and vice versa.

2. Summarize the read-aloud story in chronological order.

3. Draw a picture featuring the physical characteristics of a king and/or a knight.

Introductory Activity: Knights' Jousting Game

Materials:

- various colors of construction paper cut into 6-inch x 4-1/2-inch rectangles
- cellophane tape or safety pins

Procedure:

Have students sit in a circle facing each other. Explain that during the Middle Ages (400 to 1500 A.D.), high-ranking soldiers, who were called knights, entertained the king with fighting contests called jousts. Explain that we are going to have a contest in which no one will be hurt. Explain that you will choose two children to serve as knights. The two knights will stand in the center of the circle and close their eyes as you pin or tape a construction paper rectangle to each of their backs. Upon opening their eyes, the two knights are to move around within the circle to try and determine the color of the opponent's construction paper. The knight who successfully names his or her opponent's color wins and two other knights will be chosen to continue the game.

Recommended Books

***Conrad's Castle* by Ben Schecter** (New York: Harper & Row, 1967); full-color illustrations; Interest Level: K-3; Reading Level: 2.3.

A young boy builds an imaginary castle in the air, despite the intrusion and skepticism of his friends.

***The King at the Door* written by and pictures by Brock Cole** (New York: Doubleday & Co., 1979); full-color illustrations; Interest Level: K-3; Reading Level: 3.2.

A young boy befriends a poor man who claims to be the king and generously offers him his clothes and food while the townfolk scoff. Later, much to the surprise of everyone except the boy, the beggar indeed turns out to be the king and the boy is amply rewarded.

***The King of Kennelwick Castle* by Colin Westa, illustrated by Anne Dalton** (Philadelphia: J. B. Lippincott, 1986); full-color illustrations; Interest Level: K-3; Reading Level: 3.0.

In this cumulative rhyme, a king enjoys his rainy birthday, thanks to the local villagers.

***The King's Chessboard* by David Birch, illustrated by Devis Grebu** (New York: Dial Books, 1988); full-color illustrations; Interest Level: 3-6; Reading Level: 5.5.

A king of India insists upon rewarding a humble wise man for his service. The reward, in turn, teaches the king a valuable lesson about pride and vanity.

***The King's Commissioners* by Aileen Friedman, illustrated by Susan Guevara** (New York: Scholastic, 1995); full-color illustrations; Interest Level: K-3; Reading Level: not listed.

The king tries in vain to count his many royal commissioners until his daughter, the princess, teaches him the fundamentals of addition and multiplication.

***A Letter to the King* translated by James Anderson, story and pictures by Leong Va'** (New York: HarperCollins, 1987); full-color illustrations; Interest Level: K-3; Reading Level: 4.9.

A young Chinese girl saves her father, who is in prison, by writing and delivering a letter to the king.

***Mister King* by Raija Siekkinen, illustrated by Hannu Taina** (Minneapolis: Carolrhoda Books, 1987); full-color illustrations; Interest Level: K-3; Reading Level: 3.3.

A lonely king searches for subjects in his lovely kingdom until a cat appears on his doorstep and dissolves his loneliness.

***One Gift Deserves Another* adapted from the Brothers Grimm, by Joanne Oppenheim, illustrated by Bo Zaunders** (New York: Dutton Children's Books, 1992); full-color illustrations; Interest Level: K-3; Reading Level: 4.9.

A king rewards a poor brother for his generosity and inadvertently punishes the rich brother for his selfishness.

***Ruby the Red Knight* written and illustrated by Amy Aitken** (New York: Bradbury Press, 1983); full-color illustrations; Interest Level: K-3; Reading Level: 3.6.

A little girl imagines herself to be Ruby the Red Knight, battler of giants, dragons, and wizards.

***The Tough Princess* by Martin Waddell, illustrated by Patrick Benson** (New York: Philomel Books, 1986); full-color illustrations; Interest Level: K-3; Reading Level: 3.0.

A capable princess takes matters into her own hands when the king and queen decide that she must be married.

Nonfiction Resources

***Castle* by Christopher Gravett, photographs by Geoff Dan** (New York: Alfred A. Knopf, 1994); full-color photographs; Interest Level: 5-8; Reading Level: 6.7.

Although the text is too advanced for young children, the book presents fascinating pictures of castles, tools, clothes, and art in the Middle Ages.

***Castles* by Gallimard Jeunesse, Claude Delafosse, C. Millet and D. Millet, illustrated by C. Millet and D. Millet** (New York: Scholastic, 1990); full-color illustrations; Interest Level: K-3; Reading Level: not listed.

Using realistic illustrations and transparent overlays, the reader views the inner workings of a medieval castle.

***Kings, Queens, Knights and Jesters: Making Medieval Costumes* by Lynn Edelman Schnurnberger** (New York: Harper & Row, 1978); black-and-white photographs and illustrations, and color photographs; Interest Level: 5-8; Reading Level: 7.9.

Includes basic pattern instructions to create costumes for knight, lady sorcerer, king, and peasant, as well as accessories for each.

***A Medieval Feast* written and illustrated by Aliki** (New York: HarperCollins, 1983); full-color illustrations; Interest Level: 3-6; Reading Level: 4.0.

Beautiful illustrations and simple text describe the activities in a manor house as the residents prepare and serve a royal feast for the king.

The Ultimate Arms & Armor Sticker Book (Boston: Dorling Kindersley Book, 1995); full-color photographs; Interest and Reading Levels: not listed.

Identifies components of armor used throughout the world. Readers are to punch out armor stickers and place them on matching shapes and descriptions.

Recipe: King's Jewels

1 commercially-prepared pie crust dough package*

variety of jams such as raspberry, strawberry, and apricot

Preheat oven to 350 degrees. Use 1-1/2-inch diameter cookie cutter** to cut out circles of dough. Crimp the edges of the circles, creating a well in the middle. Place 1/8 teaspoon jam in the center of the well. Place the circles on a cookie sheet and bake for about 13 minutes or until the dough is lightly browned. Serve warm.

*Each package contains two pie crusts.

**You may make cookie cutters by cutting off the bottoms of 3-ounce plastic drinking cups.

Music Activity: "Who Is the King?" Game

Have students sit in a circle facing each other, and choose one person to be the Jack. Ask the Jack to leave the room and choose another person to serve as King (or Queen). Turn on moderately fast, appropriately majestic music—music with a clearly discernible beat.* Have the King (or Queen) show the rest of the class how to keep the beat, such as clapping hands, snapping fingers, stomping feet, etc. The rest of the class must imitate the King's (or Queen's) example. The Jack returns to the room and has three chances to guess who the King (or Queen) is. The King (or Queen), in the meantime, can change his (or her) method of keeping the beat, with the class imitating him or her when the Jack is not looking. After the Jack has exhausted his (or her) guesses or has guessed correctly, the King (or Queen) becomes the Jack and another person is chosen to be the King (or Queen).

*I recommend selected titles from an audiotape entitled *All the Best from the Pipes of Scotland*, distributed by LDMI, P.O. Box 1445, St. Laurent, Quebec, Canada H4L 4Z1.

Art Activity: King Crowns

Materials:

- photocopies of the crown pattern
- crayons
- scissors
- glue

Preparation:

Photocopy crowns, one crown per child.

Procedure:

Have students color and cut out the two pieces of the crown. Glue together the front and back sections to create a crown the children can wear.

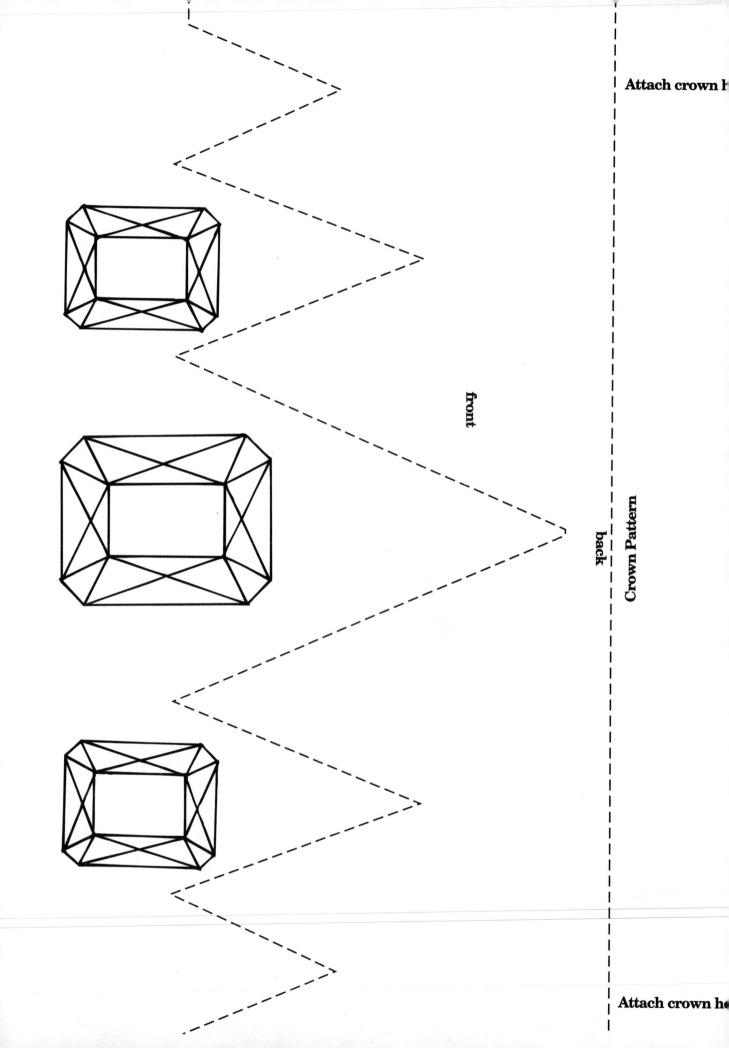

Attach crown h

front

back

Crown Pattern

Attach crown h

Name _____ Date _____

Classroom Teacher _____

Kings and Knights Research Project: Many kings are pictured holding a *scepter* and an *orb*. Look up "scepter" and "orb" in a dictionary or other reference source. Draw a scepter in one of the king's hands and an orb in the king's other hand below.

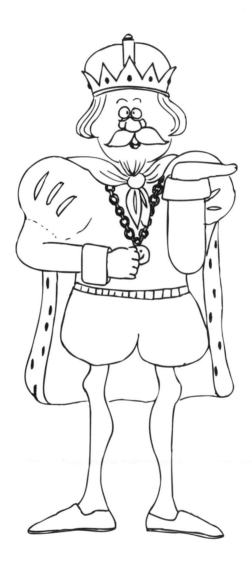

Write the title of the book where you found your information:

_____

_____

_____

Love

Getting Ready to Teach the Letter L

This unit provides a wonderful opportunity for children to bring in photos of their loved ones. The photos can be shared using a show-and-tell format and/or placed on the bulletin board decorated with hearts.

Objectives for Love :

Each child will be able to:

1. Match the letter "L" with the word "love" and vice versa.

2. Summarize the read-aloud story in chronological order.

3. Name different types of love and cite an example of each.

Introductory Activity: Screen Magic

Materials:

- four sheets of 8-1/2-inch x 11-inch white paper
- cellophane tape
- 1/2 yard non-metal screening material (available at home improvement and hardware stores) and metal cutter
- dark crayon

Preparation:

Trace the letters L,O,V, and E from the following page onto the screen and cut out. Tape the screen letters onto the chalkboard and tape a sheet of white paper over each letter.

Procedure:

When the children are assembled in front of the chalkboard, explain that you are going to say some words and they are to guess which letter begins those words. Say positive words that begin with the letter L, such as lollipops, lunch, lilies, etc. When the children guess the letter L, use the side of the crayon to color the first sheet of paper so that the letter L emerges on the paper.

Repeat the procedure for the letters O,V, and E. When LOVE has emerged, tell the students that all of the words you named are things you love. Encourage the children to talk about the things they love, too.

Recommended Books

Amelia Bedelia and the Surprise Shower **by Peggy Parish, illustrated by Fritz Siebel** (New York: HarperCollins, 1995); full-color illustrations; Interest Level: K-3; Reading Level: 2.0.

A maid named Amelia Bedelia, who literally interprets her employer's instructions, throws a surprise wedding shower. The results are humorously disastrous.

A Book of Hugs **by Dave Ross** (New York: Thomas Y. Crowell, 1980); black-and-white illustrations; Interest Level: K-3; Reading Level: 3.0.

Humorous text and illustrations identify and describe different kinds of hugs.

A Fish for Mrs. Gardenia **by Yossi Abolafia** (New York: Greenwillow Books, 1988); full-color illustrations; Interest Level: K-3; Reading Level: 3.5.

Mr. Bennett, an elderly gentleman, tries to prepare a fish dinner for his lady friend, Mrs. Gardenia, and faces a series of humorous calamities.

I Love You As Much . . . **by Laura Krauss Melmed, illustrated by Henri Sorensen** (New York: Lothrop, Lee & Shepard Books, 1993); full-color illustrations; Interest Level: K-3; Reading Level: 1.8.

Animal mothers throughout the world assure their children of their love. The book closes with a human mother tenderly loving her child.

I'll Always Love You **by Hans Wilhelm** (New York: Crown Publishers, 1985); full-color illustrations; Interest Level: K-3; Reading Level: 2.3.

A young boy recalls the love and affection of his dog, Effie, as he deals with Effie's death.

Jake Baked the Cake **by B. G. Hennessy, illustrated by Mary Morgan** (New York: Puffin Books, 1990); full-color illustrations; Interest Level: K-3; Reading Level: 1.7.

The local town is busy preparing for a wedding and Jake the baker contributes to the festivities by baking a cake.

Love You Forever **by Robert Munsch, illustrated by Sheila McGraw** (New York: Firefly Books, 1986); full-color illustrations; Interest Level: K-3; Reading Level: 4.0.

A mother cares for her child into her old age when the roles are reversed.

My Sister's Wedding **by Richard Rosenblum** (New York: William Morrow & Co., 1987); black-and-white illustrations; Interest Level: 3-6; Reading Level: 3.0.

A young Jewish girl describes the activities surrounding her sister's wedding.

The Visitors Who Came to Stay **by Annalena McAfee and Anthony Browne** (New York: Viking Kestrel, 1985); full-color illustrations; Interest Level: 3-6; Reading Level: 3.8.

After Katy's parents divorce, Katy and her dad settle into a quiet, comfortable routine until Dad's girlfriend and son move in.

The Wedding of Brown Bear and White Bear **by Martine Beck, illustrated by Marie H. Henry** (Boston: Little, Brown & Co., 1989); full-color illustrations; Interest Level: K-3; Reading Level: 2.2.

Brown Bear falls in love with White Bear and marries her in this warm, romantic tale.

Nonfiction Resources

***Daddy and Me: A Photo Story of Arthur Ashe and His Daughter Camera*, photographs and words by Jeanne Moutoussamy-Ashe** (New York: Alfred A. Knopf, 1993); black-and-white illustrations; Interest Level: K-3; Reading Level: 2.2.

The author records the love between a father and daughter and their courageous battle against the father's AIDS.

***Feelings* by Aliki** (New York: Greenwillow Books, 1984); full-color illustrations; Interest Level: K-3; Reading Level: 3.8.

Contains cartoon-like sequences, dialogs, poems, and short stories about various emotions.

***Loving* by Ann Morris, photographs by Ken Heyman** (New York: Lothrop, Lee & Shepard Books, 1990); full-color illustrations; Interest Level: K-3; Reading Level: 2.1.

Photographs of families around the world demonstrate that love comes in all colors and languages.

***Mommy Laid an Egg! or Where Do Babies Come From?* by Babette Cole** (New York: Chronicle Books, 1993); full-color illustrations; Interest Level: K-3; Reading Level: not listed.

Light, simple, humorous approach—featuring cartoon-like illustrations—describes how babies are made.

***Peace Is a Circle of Love* by Joan Walsh Anglund** (New York: Harcourt Brace Jovanovich, 1993); full-color illustrations; Interest Level: K-3; Reading Level: 3.3.

Completing the sentence "Peace is . . . ," the author defines and illustrates her definitions.

Recipe: Friendship Ice Cream

3/4 cups white sugar

2 cups half-and-half

1/2 tablespoon vanilla extract

1 cup whipping cream

1 10-ounce container of frozen, sliced strawberries, thawed and strained

approximately 8 cups crushed ice or snow

approximately 8 tablespoons rock salt or table salt

Each pint-size bag makes two servings for a total of 4 servings per recipe. Combine half-and-half, sugar, and vanilla in a large bowl. Stir until the sugar is completely dissolved. Add whipping cream and strained strawberries, and stir until blended. Divide the mixture into two 2-cup portions. Place each portion into a pint-sized plastic zip-lock bag. Fill two gallon-sized bags each with 4 cups crushed ice or snow and 4 tablespoons salt. Place a filled pint-size bag into each prepared gallon-size bag. Divide children into pairs. Wearing mittens, have each pair take turns gently rotating the gallon-sized bag until the ice cream mixture freezes, approximately 15 minutes.

Music Activity: "The Love Game"

Have students stand in a circle facing inward. Choose one person to be IT. Blindfold IT and have IT stand in the middle of the circle. Have students hold hands, walk in a clockwise direction, and sing the song. In the meantime, gently rotate IT in a counterclockwise direction. When the song is finished, everyone stands still and IT, with the blindfold still in place, points to the person facing him or her. That person says IT's name and IT has three chances to guess the identity of the child. The chosen child then becomes IT and the game continues as before.

THE LOVE GAME (Sung to the tune "Little Jack Horner.")

Art Activity: Friendship Branch

Japanese people traditionally send friendship branches to one another as a symbol of their love and good wishes. The branch is laden with tiny treasures—symbols of good luck—and other personalized mementos. Students might want to create a friendship branch for a classmate who is ill or as a thank-you to a special friend of the classroom.

Materials:

- small branch
- container in which to place the branch
- string
- cellophane tape
- hand-held paper punch
- plaster of Paris
- crayons
- safety scissors
- photocopies of friendship branch coloring page
- *optional:* shells, stones, penny candies, gumball machine toys, tiny photographs

Preparation:

Before class begins, mix the plaster of Paris per instructions on the package and pour into the container. Place the branch in the container so that it stands upright. Allow the plaster of Paris to dry completely. Photocopy the friendship branch coloring page, one paper per student. Cut the string into 6-inch lengths.

Procedure:

Have students color and cut out the designs on the coloring page. Use a paper punch to punch a hole at the top of each symbol and thread a length of string through it. Tie the string at the top and hang the ornament on the branch. For added color and fun, string beautiful stones, shells, penny candies, tiny toys, and/or small photographs from the branches, too.

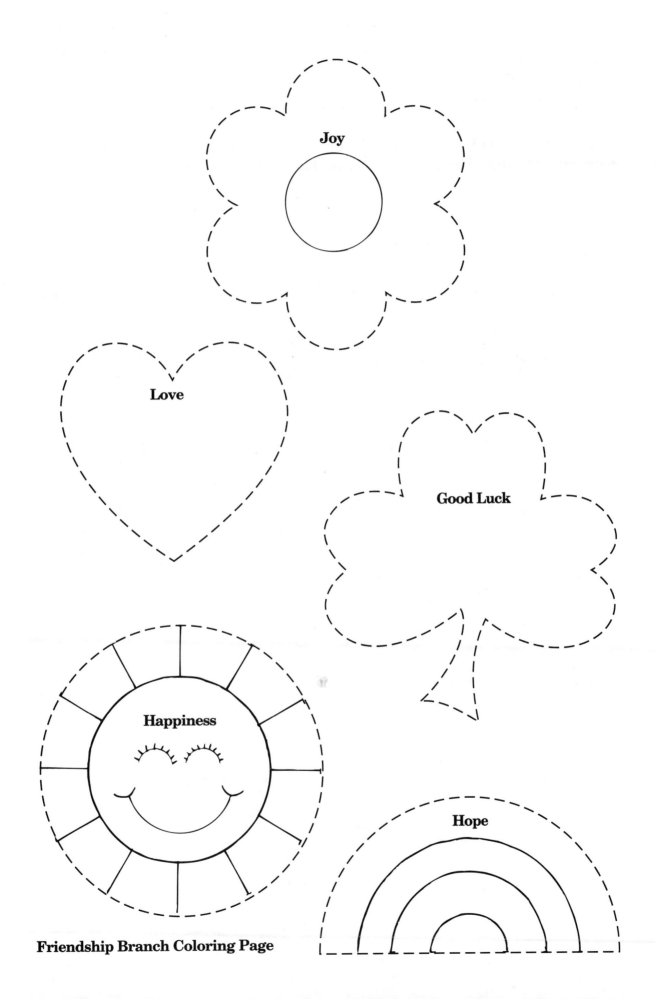

Joy

Love

Good Luck

Happiness

Hope

Friendship Branch Coloring Page

Name _____ Date _____

Classroom Teacher _____

Love Research Project: Use a rhyming dictionary to find four words that rhyme with "love" and write them on the lines below. Use those words to write a poem about love in the heart below.

1. _____ 3. _____

2. _____ 4. _____

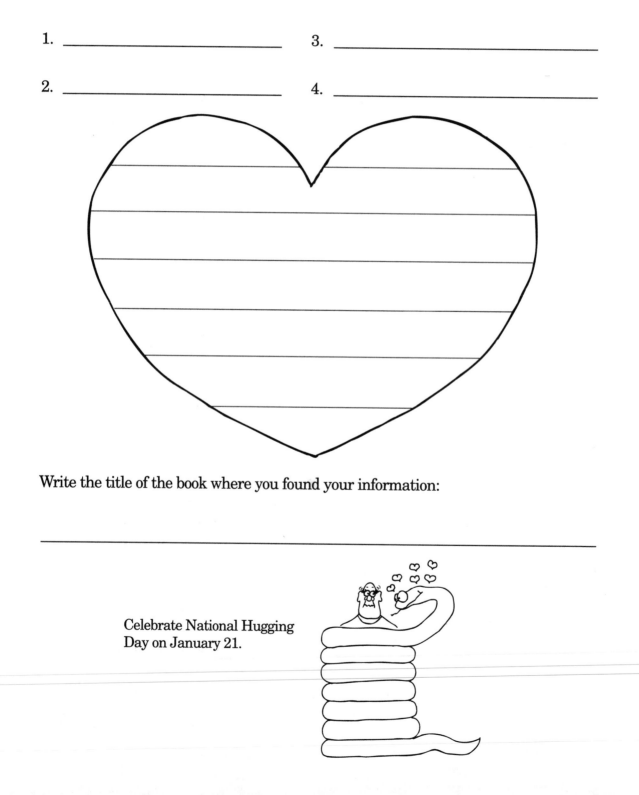

Write the title of the book where you found your information:

_____

Celebrate National Hugging
Day on January 21.

Monsters

Getting Ready to Teach the Letter M

When children are seated in the library, tell them to be on the look-out for the silliest monster they have ever seen. Describe the monster, drawing the description on a long piece of paper that has been folded in half lengthwise. At the end of the story, fold back half of the paper to reveal the word "Monster."

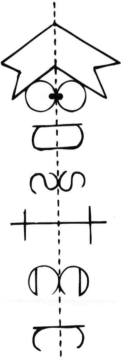

I'm going to draw a picture of a very silly monster. First of all, he has very goofy eyebrows.

He also has ridiculous eyes . . .

a crazy nose . . .

and a nutty moustache.

He also has a goofy smile . . .

a bubble chin . . .

and a turn-down collar . . .

But the silliest thing about this monster is that he spells his own name! (Fold paper in half to reveal the word "Monster.")

Objectives for Monsters:

Each child will be able to:

1. Match the letter "M" with the word "monster" and vice versa.

2. Summarize the read-aloud story in chronological order.

3. Create a picture of a monster.

Introductory Activity: Feltboard Monsters

Materials:

- felt in a variety of colors
- fabric scissors
- fabric glue
- 1 yard of cotton flannel
- monster shape patterns

Preparation:

Hang the cotton flannel on the chalkboard. Enlarge, if necessary, and cut out the shape patterns. Trace the shapes onto various colors of felt and cut out.

Procedure:

Place the egg shape in the middle of the flannel on the chalkboard. Call on individual students to choose a body part to place on the egg shape to create a monster. Several colorful monsters can be created in this way.

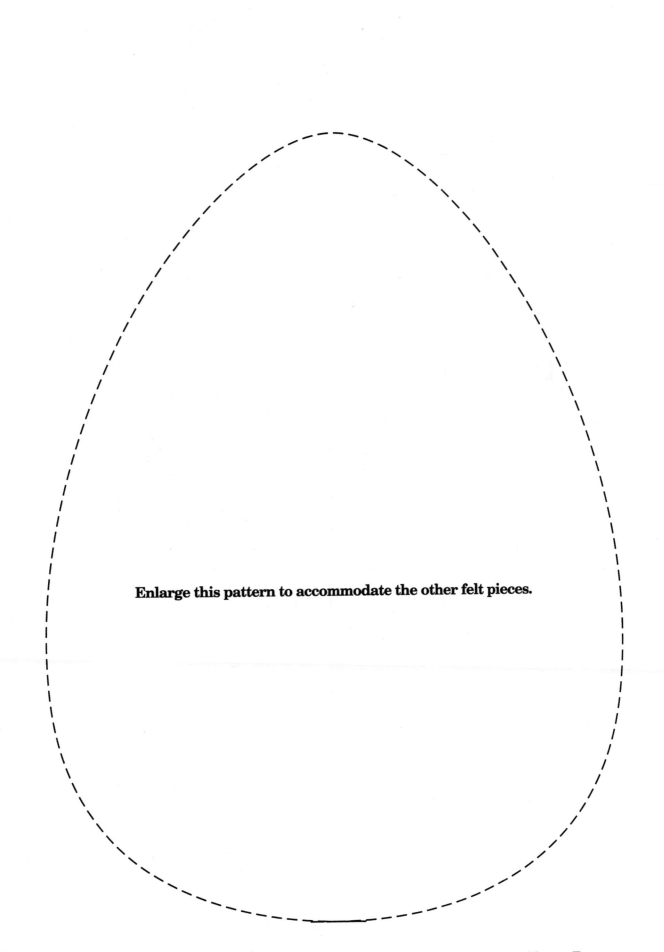

Enlarge this pattern to accommodate the other felt pieces.

Monster Shape Pattern

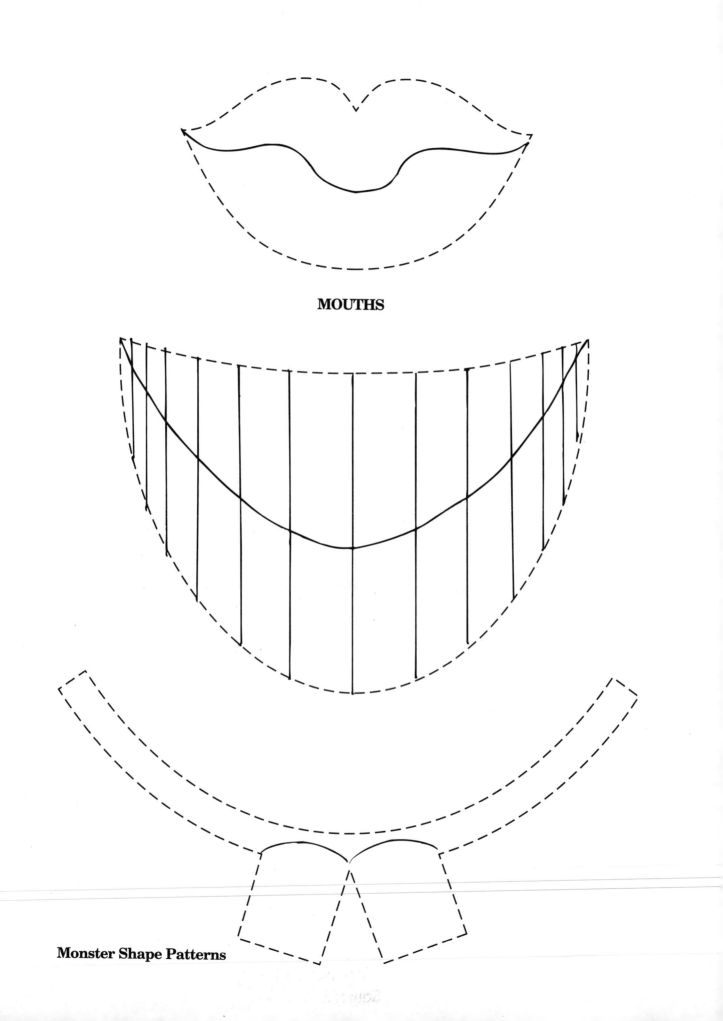

MOUTHS

Monster Shape Patterns

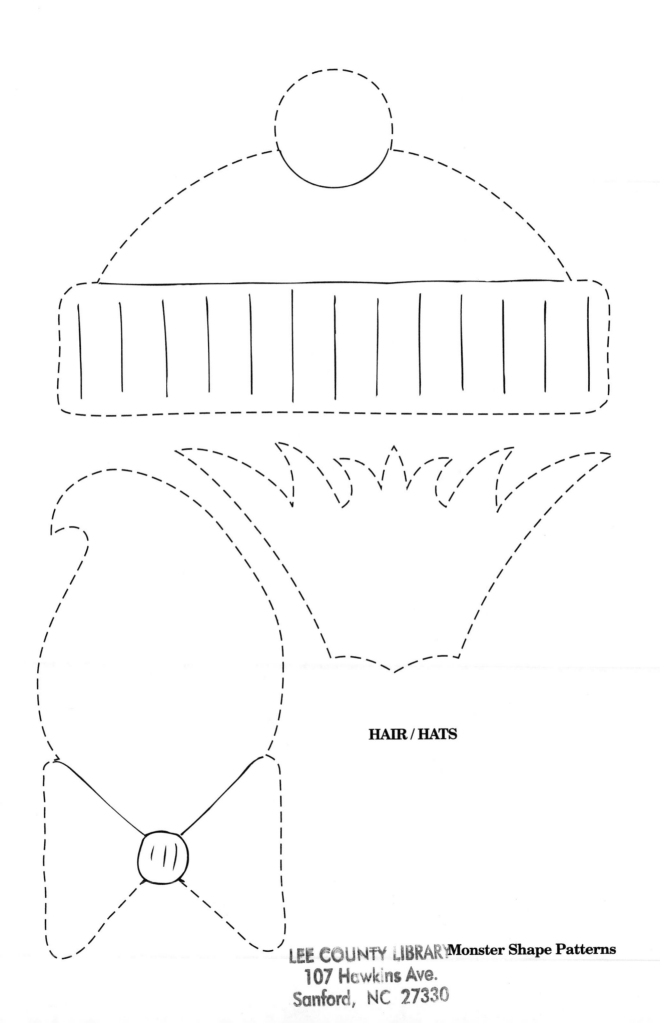

HAIR / HATS

Monster Shape Patterns

LEGS

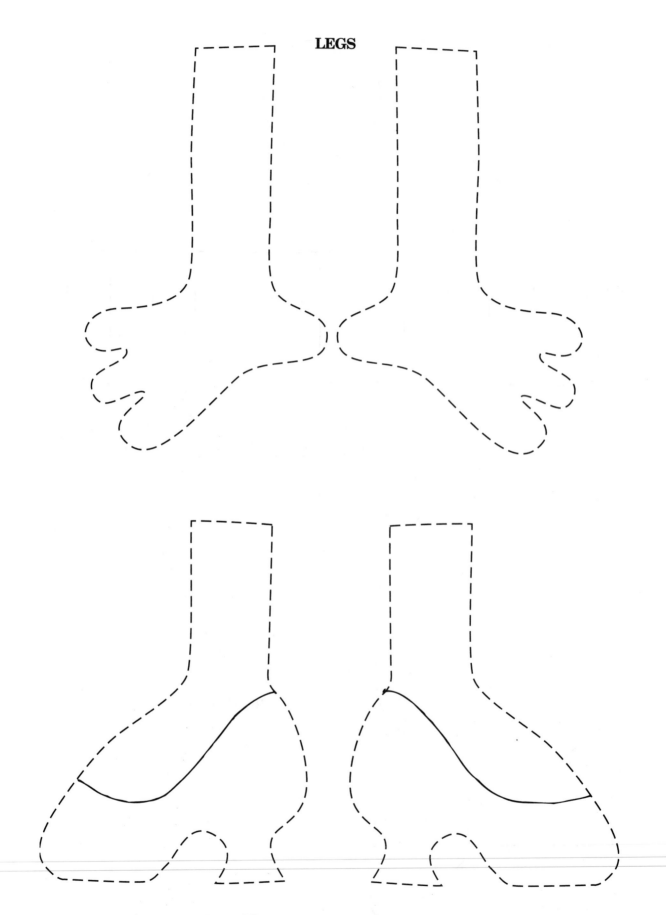

Monster Shape Patterns

LEGS

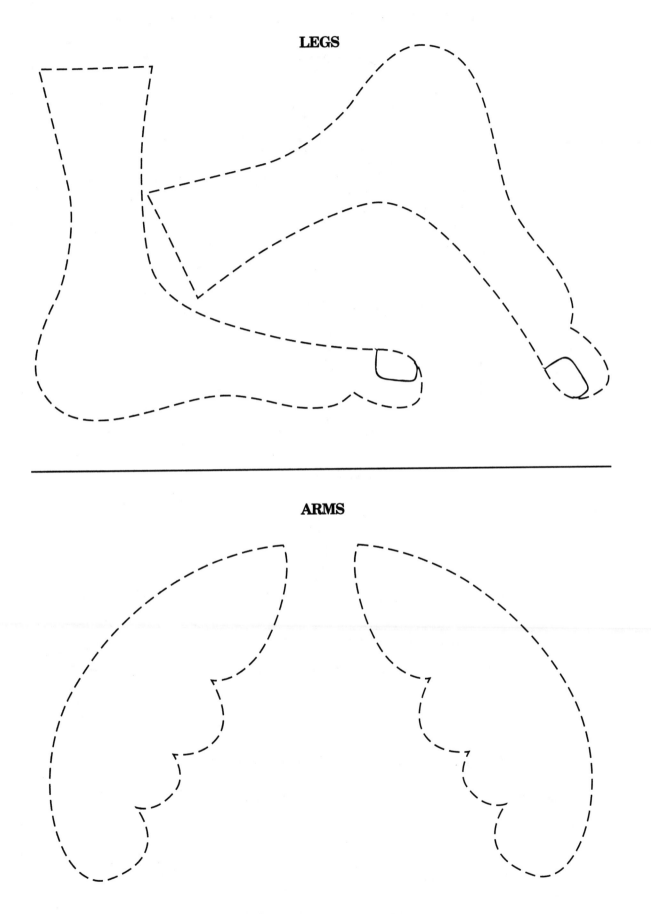

ARMS

Monster Shape Patterns

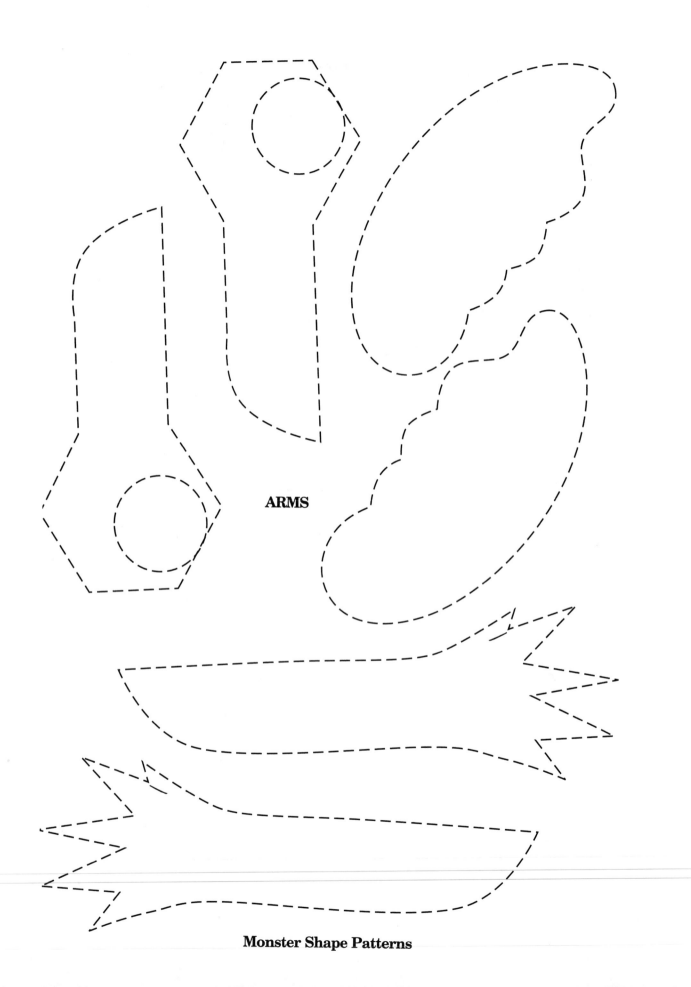

ARMS

Monster Shape Patterns

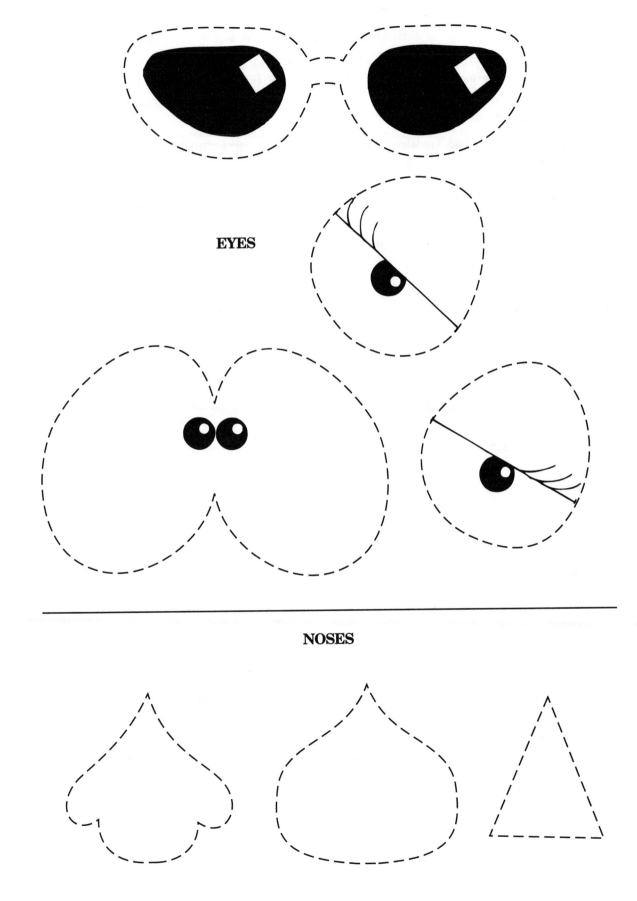

EYES

NOSES

Monster Shape Patterns

Recommended Books

***Cream of Creature from the School Cafeteria* by Mike Thayer, illustrated by Jared Lee** (New York: Avon Books, 1985); full-color illustrations; Interest Level: K-3; Reading Level: 3.0.

A green, gelatinous creature invades an elementary school. Nothing can stop it except, perhaps, a little boy named Mickey.

***Do Not Open* by Brinton Turkle** (New York: E.P. Dutton, 1981); full-color illustrations; Interest Level: K-3; Reading Level: 3.8.

A beachcomber named Miss Moody runs across a wicked genie in a bottle who threatens to unleash his bad intentions. Miss Moody, however, is not frightened and makes quick work of the creature. (This book is recommended for older readers.)

***Donovan Scares the Monsters* by Susan Love Whitlock, pictures by Yossi Abolafia** (New York: Greenwillow Books, 1987); full-color illustrations; Interest Level: K-3; Reading Level: 2.1.

A young boy named Donovan and his grandparents happily scare away the household monsters.

***Go Away Monsters, Lickety Split* by Nancy Evans Cooney, illustrated by Maxie Chambliss** (New York: G. P. Putnam's Sons, 1990); full-color illustrations; Interest Level: K-3; Reading Level: 2.3.

Jeffrey is frightened at night by unfamiliar shadows in his new house until a kitten named Lickety Split helps him overcome his fears.

***The Monster and the Tailor: A Ghost Story* by Paul Galdone** (New York: Clarion Books, 1982); full-color illustrations; Interest Level: K-3; Reading Level: 3.5.

A tailor is sewing a pair of pants for the king when he is confronted by a monster who tests his courage.

***The Monster Under My Bed* by Suzanne Gruber, illustrated by Stephanie Britt** (Mahwah, NJ: Troll Associates, 1985); full-color illustrations; Interest Level: K-3; Reading Level: 1.6.

A little bear imagines a scary monster under his bed until he discovers his cat, Fluffy, is making the scary noises.

***Mr. Monster* by William H. Hooks, illustrated by Paul Meisel** (New York: Bantam, Doubleday, Dell, 1990); full-color illustrations; Interest Level: K-3; Reading Level: 2.5.

Five-year-old Eli loves his toy monsters but his brother and their friend plot to rid Eli's room of his favorite toys.

***There's a Nightmare in My Closet* written and illustrated by Mercer Mayer** (New York: Dial Books, 1968/1990); two-color illustrations; Interest Level: pre-3; Reading Level: 3.4.

A young boy is afraid of the monsters in his closet until he finds the lovable monsters are more frightened than he is.

***The Very Worst Monster* by Pat Hutchins** (New York: Greenwillow Books, 1985); full-color illustrations; Interest Level: K-3; Reading Level: 2.2.

Hazel Monster is jealous of her baby brother and decides to proves that she's the best monster in the world.

***Where the Wild Things Are* written and illustrated by Maurice Sendak** (New York: HarperCollins, 1963/1984/1992); full-color illustrations; Interest Level: K-3; Reading Level: 4.4.

When a young boy named Max is sent to his room as punishment, he takes an imaginary trip to the land of the Wild Things.

Nonfiction Resources

Do-It-Yourself Monster Make-Up **by Dick Smith** (New York: Harmony Books, 1985); black-and-white and color photographs; Interest and Reading Levels: not listed.

Presents step-by-step instructions for creating faces of a ghoul, werewolf, martian, mummy, and other ghastly creatures.

Happy Haunting: Halloween Costumes You Can Make **by Judith Conaway, illustrated by Renzo Barto** (Mahwah, NJ: Troll Associates, 1986); three-color illustrations; Interest Level: K-3; Reading Level: 3.3.

Contains simple instructions for 17 costume ideas.

Horrorgami: Spooky Paperfolding Just for Fun **by Richard Saunders and Brian Mackness** (New York: Sterling Publishing Co., 1992); one-color illustrations; Interest Level: 3-6; Reading Level: 5.6.

Contains instructions for 11 spooky creatures and objects using basic origami folds.

I Didn't Know That! about Strange but True Mysteries **by Anthony Tallarico** (Chicago: Kidsbooks, 1992); full-color illustrations; Interest and Reading Levels: not listed.

Readers find a list of hidden items among illustrations of famous mysteries including the Loch Ness Monster, Bigfoot, and the Giant Statues of Easter Island.

Monsters of the Mountains **by Jon Jameson, illustrated by Steven Marches** (New York: Franklin Watts, 1980); full-color and black-and-white illustrations; Interest Level: K-3; Reading Level: 2.8.

Tells the legends and known facts about Bigfoot, Alma, Yeti, and other creatures.

Recipe: Monster Pizza

6 English muffins, split

1 15-ounce can pizza sauce

1 small bag sliced pepperoni

1 8-ounce bag shredded Mozzarella cheese

1 green pepper, sliced

1 4-ounce can mushrooms, drained

1 6-ounce can olives, drained

This recipe makes 12 pizzas. Brown the English muffins in a toaster or toaster oven. Spread one tablespoon of pizza sauce on each muffin half. Using the toppings listed above, create a monster face. Place the muffins on a cookie sheet and bake in a preheated 350° oven for 15 to 20 minutes or until the cheese melts.

Music Activity: "The Monster Song"

See additional verses and finger plays on the following page.

THE MONSTER SONG
(Sung to the tune "She'll Be Coming 'Round the Mountain.")

If you're a mon–ster and you know it, grunt and

groan, (UGH) (UGH). If you're a mon–ster and you

know it, grunt and groan, (UGH) (UGH). If you're

a mon–ster and you know it, then you sur– ly ought to

show it. If you're a mon– ster and you know it, grunt and

groan, (UGH) (UGH).

Verse 2:   If you're a monster and you know it,
Flail your arms (swish, swish).
If you're a monster and you know it,
Flail your arms (swish, swish).
If you're a monster and you know it,
Then you surely ought to show it.
If you're a monster and you know it,
Flail your arms (swish, swish).

(Flail arms.)

Verse 3:   If you're a monster and you know it,
Stomp your feet (stomp, stomp).
If you're a monster and you know it,
Stomp your feet (stomp, stomp).
If you're a monster and you know it,
Then you surely ought to show it.
If you're a monster and you know it,
Stomp your feet (stomp, stomp).

(Stomp feet.)

Verse 4:   If you're a monster and you know it,
Make a face.
If you're a monster and you know it,
Make a face.
If you're a monster and you know it,
Then you surely ought to show it.
If you're a monster and you know it,
Make a face.

(Make a face.)

Verse 5:   If you're a monster and you know it,
Do all four.
If you're a monster and you know it,
Do all four.
If you're a monster and you know it,
Then you surely ought to show it.
If you're a monster and you know it,
Do all four.

*(Grunt and groan, flail arms,
stomp feet, and make a face.)*

Art Activity: Monster Hat

Materials:

- photocopies of the hat pattern (one copy per child)
- crayons
- safety scissors
- tape or stapler
- *optional:* stickers, paper punches, cotton balls, posterboard, construction paper, aluminum foil, etc.

Procedure:

Have students cut out and tape or staple the hat's front and back together. Using crayons and possibly other found items, such as cotton balls, paper punches, etc., have students decorate their hats to resemble an outer space creature.

For added fun, use fluorescent crayons instead of regular crayons. At the end of class, turn off all lights, turn on a black light, and have students watch their creations glow in the dark. (Black light bulbs are available at novelty stores and mail order catalogs, and screw into regular light fixtures.)

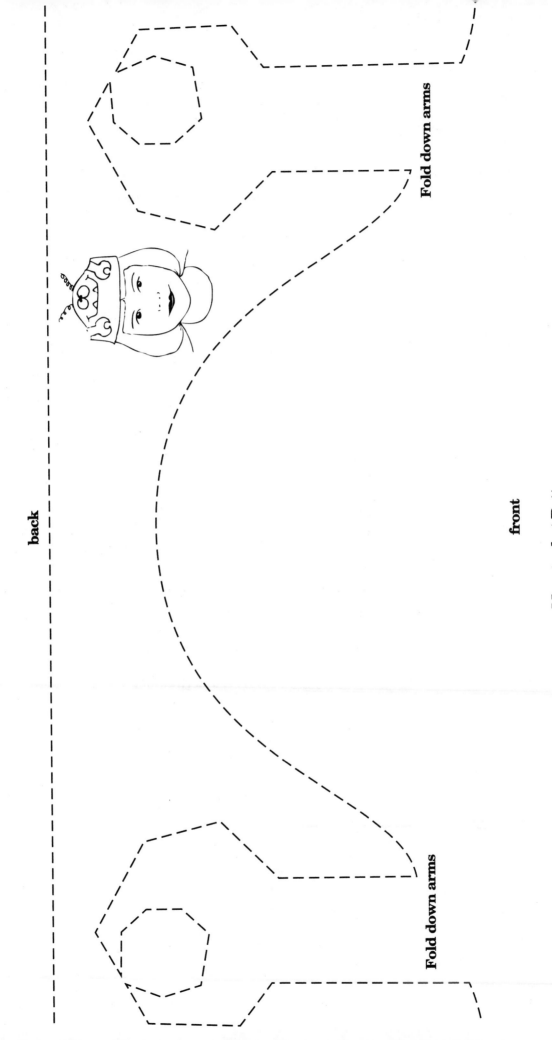

back

Fold down arms

Fold down arms

front

Monster hat Pattern

Name _____ Date _____

Classroom Teacher _____

Monsters Research Project: Look up "gila monster" in an encyclopedia or other reference source. Draw a picture of a gila monster in the space below.

Write the title of the book where you found your information:

_____

Monster Ballet

Nighttime

Getting Ready to Teach the Letter N

A week before beginning this lesson, send the following note home to parents and guardians asking their child to dress in pajamas for the nighttime lesson. You should also dress in pajamas or a bathrobe for the occasion. When the children enter the library, the lights should be turned low and lullabies should be playing on the tape recorder.

Dear Parents and Guardians,

Next week, we will study the key word NIGHTTIME. We plan to celebrate this word with a library slumber party. We will play a nighttime game, read a bedtime story, and create a lullaby craft. We invite your child to add to the fun by wearing his or her pajamas to library class and/or bringing a favorite stuffed animal or blanket.

Objectives for Nighttime:
Each child will be able to:

1. Match the letter "N" with the word "nighttime" and vice versa.

2. Summarize the read-aloud story in chronological order.

3. Identify the characteristics of nighttime.

Introductory Activity: Find a Falling Star

Materials:

- foil star stickers
- colored paper or posterboard
- *optional:* a small prize such as an eraser or pencil

Preparation:

Cut the colored paper or posterboard into 1-inch squares. Place a star on each square and hide the squares throughout the library. (For more fun, hide glow-in-the-dark stars.) Ready-made stars are available at many variety stores. For homemade stars, glow-in-the-dark paper and star paper punches are available from Accucut, 1035 East Dodge Street, P.O. Box 1053, Fremont, Nebraska 68025; 1-800-288-1670.

Procedure:

Turn down the lights just before the students enter the library. Explain to the children that falling nighttime stars have landed in the library. The children are to find as many stars as possible within a 5-minute time period. Remind the children that when you call "time," they are to return to their seats and count the stars they found. *Optional:* Award a prize to the child who found the greatest number of stars.

Recommended Books

***Asleep, Asleep* by Mira Ginsburg, illustrated by Nancy Tafuri** (New York: Greenwillow Books, 1992); full-color illustrations; Interest Level: K-3; Reading Level: 1.5.

A mother coos a nighttime poem to her sleepy baby.

***Aunt Nina, Good Night* by Franz Brandenberg, illustrated by Aliki** (New York: Greenwillow Books, 1989); full-color illustrations; Interest Level: K-3; Reading Level: 1.5.

Aunt Nina's nieces and nephews spend the night, changing the sleeping arrangements and finding excuses for staying awake.

***The Dream Child* by David McPhail** (New York: E.P. Dutton, 1985); full-color illustrations; Interest Level: K-3; Reading Level: 2.0.

A young girl, the Dream Child, and her teddy bear sail into a land of magical adventures.

***Dreamcatcher* by Audrey Osofsky, illustrated by Ed Young** (New York: Orchard Books, 1992); full-color illustrations; Interest Level: K-3; Reading Level: 4.6.

A gentle, free-form poem lulls an Ojibwa baby to sleep.

***Harry's Night Out* by Abigail Pizer** (New York: Dial Books, 1987); full-color illustrations; Interest Level: K-3; Reading Level: 3.0.

Harry the cat goes on nocturnal hunts, although his owner thinks Harry sleeps throughout the night.

***I Hear a Noise* by Diane Goode** (New York: E.P. Dutton, 1988); full-color illustrations; Interest Level: K-3; Reading Level: 2.0.

A friendly bedtime monster picks up a young boy and his mother, takes them to his home, and then gently returns them to their own home.

In the Night **by Jonathan Shipton, illustrated by Gill Scriven** (Boston: Little, Brown and Company, 1987/1992); full-color illustrations; Interest Level: K-3; Reading Level: 3.5.

A little girl wakes in the middle of the night to watch and listen to the sights and sounds of the dark.

Moon Tiger **by Phyllis Root, illustrated by Ed Young** (New York: Holt, Rinehart and Winston, 1985); full-color illustrations; Interest Level: K-3; Reading Level: 3.1.

A young girl, who is sent to bed early for disobeying her mother, imagines riding through the night with a powerful yet friendly moon tiger.

Pajama Walking **by Vicki Kimmel Artis, illustrated by Emily Arnold McCully** (Boston: Houghton Mifflin, 1981); two-color illustrations; Interest Level: K-3; Reading Level: 2.6.

In this four-part story, two best friends experience a series of misadventures when they sleep together overnight.

Somebody's Sleepy **by Paul Rogers, illustrated by Robin Bell** (New York: Antheneum, 1988); full-color illustrations; Interest Level: K-3; Reading Level: 1.6.

A young boy declares he is not sleepy, although he can't stay awake long enough for his mother to read him a bedtime story.

Nonfiction Resources

Animals Sleeping **by Masayuki Yabuuchi** (New York: Philomel Books, 1981); full-color illustrations; Interest Level: K-3; Reading Level: 2.4.

Illustrations and simple text explain how six animals sleep. Those animals include a flamingo, leopard, bat, sea otter, albatross, and camel.

Glow-in-the-Dark Constellations: A Field Guide for Young Stargazers **by C. E. Thompson, illustrations by Randy Chewing** (New York: Grosset & Dunlap, 1989); full-color and glow-in-the-dark illustrations; Interest and Reading Levels: not listed.

Glow-in-the-dark stars and text explain locations, legends, and information about twelve constellations.

The Stars: Lights in the Night Sky **by Jeanne Bendick, illustrated by Chris Forsey** (Brookfield, CT: Millbrook Press, 1991); Interest Level: K-3; Reading Level: 4.6.

Explains the formations and types of constellations.

What Makes Day and Night **by Franklyn M. Branley, illustrated by Arthur Dorros** (New York: Thomas Y. Crowell, 1961/1986); full-color illustrations; Interest Level: K-3; Reading Level: 2.3.

Illustrations and simple text explain how and why day turns into night and vice versa.

What Happens When You Sleep **by Joy Richardson, illustrated by Colin and Moira Maclean** (New York: Gareth Stevens Publishing, 1984); full-color illustrations; Interest Level: K-3; Reading Level: 4.3.

Simple text explains the process of sleeping in the human body.

Recipe: Dream Bars

2 cups graham cracker crumbs

1 cup brown sugar

1 cup (2 sticks) butter

1 cup chopped walnuts

1 cup chocolate chips

1 cup shredded coconut

This recipe makes about 18 2-inch x 3-inch bars. Preheat oven to 350 degrees. Melt butter in a saucepan. Add sugar and stir until melted. In a bowl, mix the butter, sugar, and graham crackers. Spread into a greased 13-inch x 9-inch pan. Top with chocolate chips, coconut, and walnuts. Bake for 10 minutes. When cool, cut into bars.

Music Activity: "Don't Wake the Baby"

You will need a hand-held kitchen timer for this activity. Have children sit in a circle facing each other. Set the timer at 30 to 60 seconds. Have students begin passing the timer around the circle while continuously singing the song. When the timer rings, the person holding the timer has "awakened the baby" and must sit outside the circle. The game may continue until one player is left.

DON'T WAKE THE BABY (Sung to the tune "Pop Goes the Weasel.")

Art Activity: The Sweet Dream Fairy

This Sweet Dream Fairy, when completed, can be placed by a child's bed to chase away bad dreams and encourage sweet dreams.

Materials:

- Sweet Dream Fairy pattern
- cotton balls dyed brown, black, yellow, and/or orange **OR** colored yarn (brown, black, yellow, and/or orange) cut into 1-inch lengths
- crayons
- safety scissors
- glue
- *optional:* glitter, rick-rack, lace, ribbon, etc.

Preparation:

Photocopy the Sweet Dream Fairy pattern (one copy per child). Dye cotton balls the color of hair or cut colored yarn into 1-inch lengths.

Procedure:

Have students pull apart and fluff the cotton balls or yarn. Color and cut out the fairy. Glue hair to the fairy's head. Turn down the two corners on the fairy (marked with an X) to the X in the middle and glue in place. *Optional:* Decorate the fairy with glitter, ribbon, rick-rack, etc.

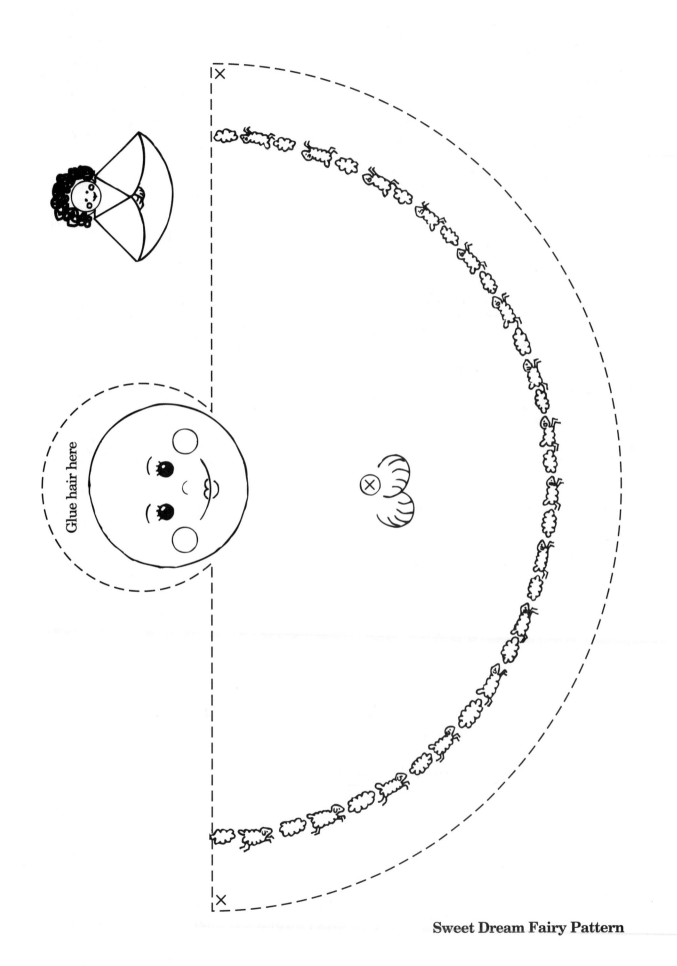

Glue hair here

Sweet Dream Fairy Pattern

Name _____ Date _____

Classroom Teacher _____

Nighttime Research Project: Look up "moon" in an encyclopedia or other reference source. In each box below, shade the moon to represent each phase.

◯ New Moon	◯ Waxing Crescent	◯ First Quarter	◯ Waxing Gibbous
◯ Full Moon	◯ Waning Gibbous	◯ Last Quarter	◯ Waning Crescent

Write the title of the book where you found your information:

_____

_____

_____

Neil Armstrong was the first human being to walk on the moon.
He made his historic journey on July 20, 1969.

Outer Space

Getting Ready to Teach the Letter O

Decorate the room for a simulated space flight by stringing tiny white Christmas tree lights onto the ceiling. Make sound effects for a space shuttle leaving and entering Earth's atmosphere by tape recording an electric mixer or vacuum cleaner running at various speeds. You may want to dress in a white sweat suit and, as students enter the room, ask them to crawl through a tunnel or box. Before you begin to read the story, tell students that we are going to travel into outer space. Our assignment, once we are in orbit, is to read a book, then descend to Earth. Also warn students that there will be a momentary blackout as we leave Earth's atmosphere. When we are ready to begin, start the tape recording, turn off all overhead lights, and turn on the Christmas lights, which represent stars. When finished reading the book, play a recording of the electric mixer (or vacuum cleaner) gradually being turned off while, at the same time, turning off the Christmas lights and turning on the overhead lights.

Objectives for Outer Space:

Each child will be able to:

1. Match the letter "O" with the word "outer space" and vice versa.

2. Summarize the read-aloud story in chronological order.

3. Draw a picture of outer space featuring common space objects such as stars, planets, asteroids, and satellites.

Introductory Activity: Outer Space Drawing Story

This is a story about (*child's name*). (*Child's name*) loves to think about outer space. As soon as (*child's name*) gets off the bus in the afternoon, he (or she) rushes to his (or her) room to look at his (or her) telescope. The telescope is long and thin with buttons at the bottom to adjust the machine.

(*Child's name*) enjoys looking at the tiny stars in the skies.

Sometimes (*child's name*) sees planets through his (or her) telescope.

Sometimes he (or she) even sees an asteroid traveling through space.

One day, (*child's name*) was so busy looking through his (or her) telescope that he (or she) forgot to eat his (or her) dinner. His (or her) dad took a bowl of soup to (*child's name*)'s room so he (or she) wouldn't go hungry.

As (*child's name*) continued to look through the telescope, he (or she) saw something in the middle of the skies that amazed him (or her). What did (*child's name*) see?

Recommended Books

***Blast Off! Poems about Space* selected by Lee Bennett Hopkins, illustrated by Melissa Sweet** (New York: HarperCollins, 1995); full-color illustrations; Interest Level: K-3; Reading Level: 3.5.

Contains twenty short poems by different authors about outer space.

***Builder of the Moon* by Tim Wynne-Jones, illustrated by Ian Wallace** (New York: Margaret K. McElderry Books, 1988); full-color illustrations; Interest Level: K-3; Reading Level: not listed.

A young boy takes a quick trip into outer space to repair the moon.

***Cabbage Moon* by Jan Wahl, illustrated by Adrienne Adams** (New York: Holt, Rinehart and Winston, 1965); full-color illustrations; Interest Level: K-3; Reading Level: not listed.

A princess and her dog free the moon after it is stolen by a miser.

***Commander Toad and the Big Black Hole* by Jane Yolen, illustrated by Bruce Degen** (New York: Coward-McCann, 1983); black-and-white and two-color illustrations; Interest Level: K-3; Reading Level: 2.5.

Commander Toad and his silly yet loyal crew escape from a giant Extra Terrestrial Toad.

***Guys from Space* by Daniel Pinkwater** (New York: Aladdin Books, 1989); full-color illustrations; Interest Level: K-3; Reading Level: 2.5.

A young boy takes a trip in a spaceship with friendly aliens to a distant planet and returns home to his unsuspecting mother.

***Mooncake* by Frank Asch** (Englewood Cliffs, NJ: Prentice-Hall, 1983); full-color illustrations; Interest Level: K-3; Reading Level: 2.4.

Bear falls asleep in his homemade spacecraft and awakes to find himself on what he believes to be the moon's surface.

***Space Case* by Edward Marshall, illustrated by James Marshall** (New York: Dial Books, 1980); full-color illustrations; Interest Level: K-3; Reading Level: 3.3.

A lovable creature from outer space lands on Earth and makes friends with a boy named Buddy. They go trick-or-treating together.

***Space Songs* by Myra Cohn Livingston, illustrated by Leonard Everett Fisher** (New York: Holiday House, 1988); full-color illustrations; Interest Level: K-3; Reading Level: 4.1.

Contains thirteen poems about objects in outer space.

***Trouble in Space* by Rose Greyanus, illustrated by Don Page** (Mahwah, NJ: Troll Associates, 1981); full-color illustrations; Interest Level: K-3; Reading Level: 1.5.

Teddy blasts into outer space and, when trouble arises, parachutes to safety.

***UFO Diary* by Satoshi Kitamura** (New York: Farrar, Straus, Giroux, 1989); full-color illustrations; Interest Level: K-3; Reading Level: 3.0.

A young boy befriends a visiting UFO and together they explore Earth.

Nonfiction Resources

***Can You Hitch a Ride on a Comet?* by Sidney Rosen, illustrated by Dean Lindberg** (Minneapolis: Carolrhoda Books, 1993); Interest Level: K-3; Reading Level: 3.9.

A young boy learns about the origin, composition, and cycle of a comet by asking questions.

***Making Space Puppets* written and illustrated by Dave Ross** (New York: Franklin Watts, 1980); two-color illustrations; Interest Level: K-3; Reading Level: 5.5.

Contains instructions for creating unidentified moving objects using everyday materials.

***Now I Know Stars* by Roy Wandelmaier, illustrated by Irene Trivas** (Mahwah, NJ: Troll Associates, 1985); full-color illustrations; Interest and Reading Levels: not listed.

Using simple text and colorful illustrations, the author explains different types of stars.

***The Sky Is Full of Stars* by Franklyn M. Branley, illustrated by Felicia Bond** (New York: HarperCollins, 1983); black-and-white and two-color illustrations; Interest Level: K-3; Reading Level: 4.0.

Introduces basic astronomy and legends about the stars.

***Which Way to the Milky Way?* by Sidney Rosen, illustrated by Dean Lindberg** (Minneapolis: Carolrhoda Books, 1992); full-color illustrations; Interest Level: K-3; Reading Level: 3.5.

Cartoon-like characters pose questions and learn answers about the Milky Way and other galaxies.

Recipe: Asteroids

1 pound seasoned sausage, crumbled and browned, drained and cooled

1 pound (16 ounces) mild grated cheddar cheese

1 cup biscuit baking mix

This recipe makes about 18 balls. Preheat oven to 350 degrees. Mix ingredients together. Roll into 1-1/2-inch balls. Bake for 25 minutes. Serve warm.

Music Activity: "Earth"

Using the accompanying verses, cut out the letters and five circles from felt. When the song begins, place the letters EARTH on a felt board. As the song is sung, point to each letter as it is named. At the end of each verse, replace each letter, beginning with E and ending with H, with a circle. The circle signifies a clap. Point to the letters and circles through the last verse when all the letters have been replaced with circles.

EARTH (Sung to the tune "Bingo.")

Verse 2: There are nine planets that circle the sun,
And Earth is third from the center.
(*Clap*)-A-R-T-H, (*clap*)-A-R-T-H, (*clap*)-A-R-T-H,
And Earth is third from the center.

Verse 3: There are nine planets that circle the sun,
And Earth is third from the center.
(*Clap, clap*)-R-T-H, (*clap, clap*)-R-T-H, (*clap, clap*)-R-T-H,
And Earth is third from the center.

Verse 4: There are nine planets that circle the sun,
And Earth is third from the center.
(*Clap, clap, clap*)-T-H, (*clap, clap, clap*)-T-H, (*clap, clap, clap*)-T-H,
And Earth is third from the center.

Verse 5: There are nine planets that circle the sun,
And Earth is third from the center.
(*Clap, clap, clap, clap*)-H, (*clap, clap, clap, clap*)-H, (*clap, clap, clap, clap*)-H,
And Earth is third from the center.

Verse 6: There are nine planets that circle the sun,
And Earth is third from the center.
(*Clap, clap, clap, clap, clap*), (*clap, clap, clap, clap, clap*), (*clap, clap, clap, clap, clap*),
And Earth is third from the center.

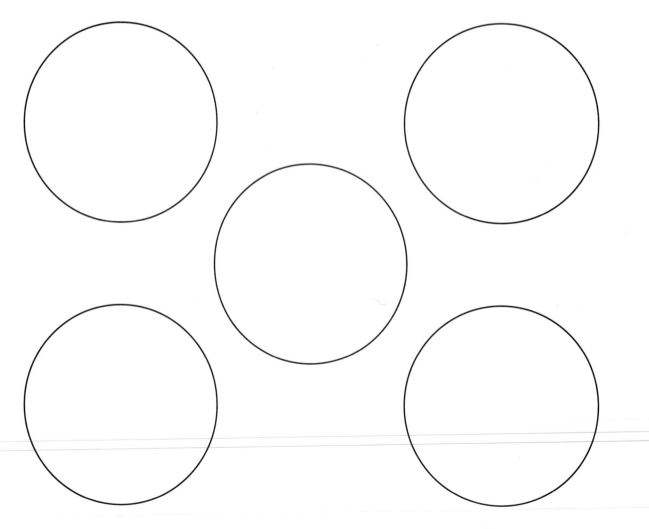

Art Activity: Constellation Drawing

Materials:

- pencils (one per child)
- photocopies of the constellation patterns (one set of constellations per child)

Preparation:

Photocopy the constellations.

Procedure:

Explain to the students that ancient astronomers, or star gazers from long ago, imagined that groups of stars formed pictures of animals, heroes, and objects. They called these groups of stars *constellations*. Explain that the class will draw a few of these constellations by completing the pictures using a dot-to-dot, or more accurately, a star-to-star method. Hand out the constellation pictures and have students complete the pictures by connecting the stars in numerical order. Remind the students that the same constellations they are drawing can be found in the skies on a clear night.

Little Dipper (Ursa Minor)

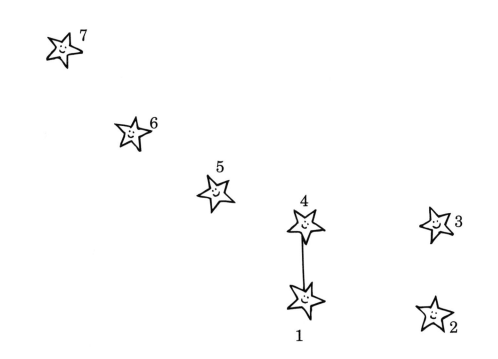

Great Dog (Canis Major)

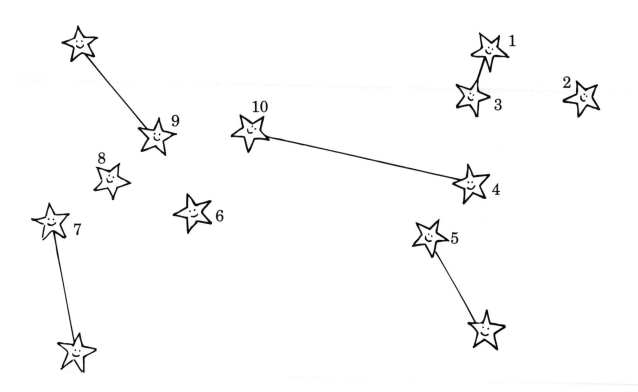

Dragon (Draco)

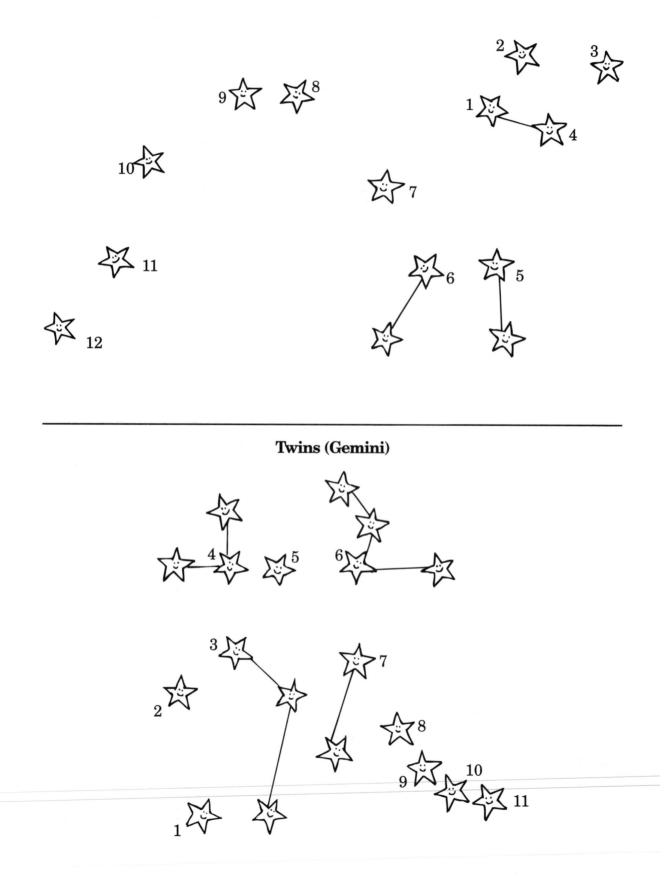

Twins (Gemini)

Name _____ Date _____

Classroom Teacher _____

Outer Space Research Project: Look up "planets" in an encyclopedia or other reference book. Label each of the planets below.

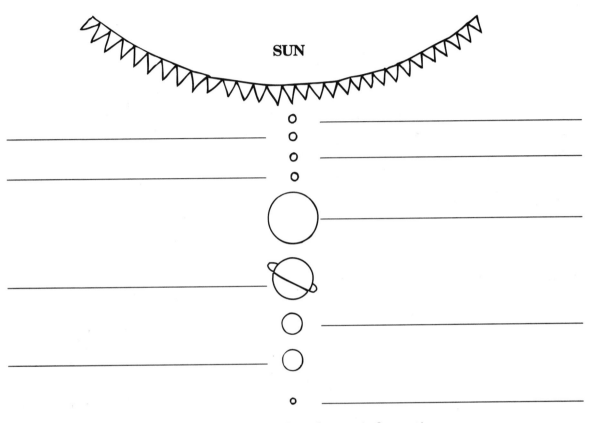

SUN

Write the title of the book where you found your information:

_____

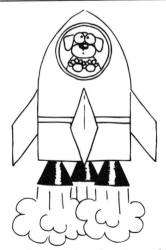

Laika was the first animal to travel into outer space.
The dog was launched on November 3, 1957 from Russia.

Pirates

Getting Ready to Teach the Letter P

It is easy to dress as a pirate using regular household items. A T-shirt, preferably red and white striped, with a pair of jeans, rolled to the knees, white stockings, and loafers can serve as the costume. Other accessories include a red bandana tied around the head, a gold hoop earring, and a few scars drawn with eyeliner pencil. Background music might include Irish reels and/or an audio recording of the ocean surf.

Objectives for Pirates:

Each child will be able to:

1. Match the letter "P" with the word "pirate" and vice versa.

2. Summarize the read-aloud story in chronological order.

3. Define and describe a pirate.

Introductory Activity: Hidden Treasure

Materials:

- aluminum foil, cut or ripped into 2-inch squares
- the treasure map (provided)
- *optional:* 12-inch length of ribbon

Preparation:

Crumple aluminum foil squares into small balls and hide them throughout the library. Photocopy the treasure map, roll it up, and tie it with a ribbon. (For added effect, spritz the map with diluted coffee or tea to give it an aged effect, let dry, color the landmarks, and tear the paper edges.)

Procedure:

Explain that you were cleaning your attic a few days ago when you came across a sea chest. When you opened the chest, you found a treasure map. (Show children the map.) Explain that according to the map, there is a treasure of silver nuggets hidden throughout the library. Give the children five minutes to find the "nuggets" and return to their seats.

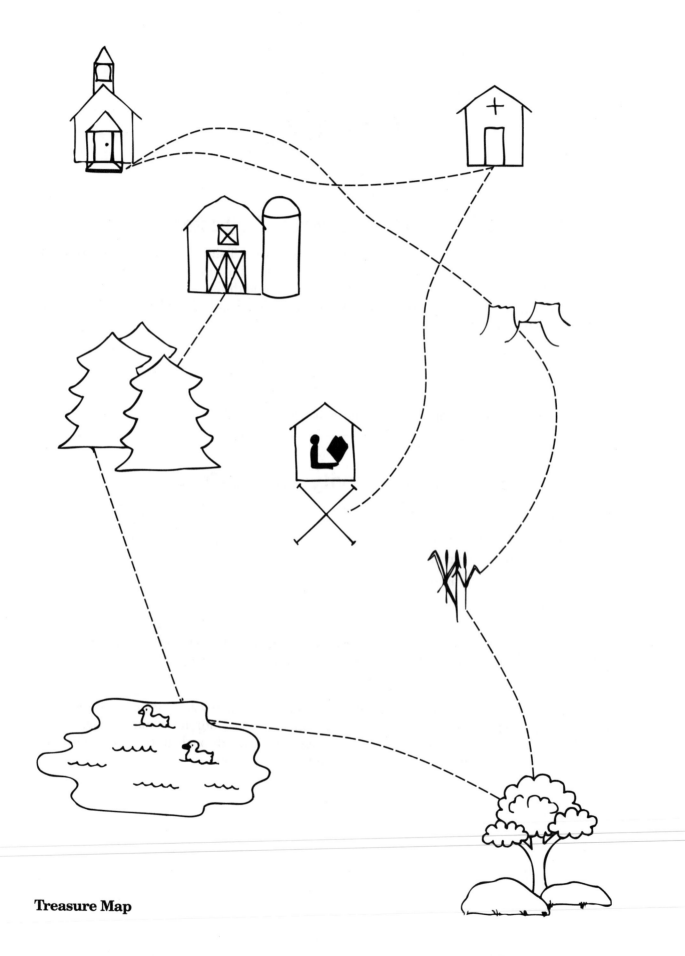

Treasure Map

Recommended Books

***The Ballad of the Pirate Queens* by Jane Yolen, illustrated by David Shannon** (San Diego: Harcourt Brace & Co., 1995); full-color illustrations; Interest Level: 3-6; Reading Level: 6.2.

Presents, in rhyme, the legend of Anne Bonney and Mary Reade, two infamous female pirates.

***Do Pirates Take Baths?* by Kathy Tucker, illustrated by Nadine Bernard Westcott** (New York: Albert Whitman & Co., 1994); full-color illustrations; Interest Level: K-3; Reading Level: 1.7.

Contains whimsical, short poems about different aspects of friendly pirate life.

***Grandma and the Pirates* by Phoebe Gilman** (New York: Scholastic, 1990); full-color illustrations; Interest Level: K-3; Reading Level: 2.7.

A merry band of pirates kidnap Grandma and her two grandchildren, but the children devise a plan to escape.

***The Man Whose Mother Was a Pirate* by Margaret Mahy, illustrated by Margaret Chamberlain** (New York: Puffin Books, 1972/1985); full-color illustrations; Interest Level: 3-6; Reading Level: 4.1.

A mousy bank clerk takes his mother, a former pirate, to the sea where they joyfully join a pirate ship.

***The Mystery of the Pirate Ghost* by Geoffrey Hayes** (New York: Random House, 1985); full-color illustrations; Interest Level: K-3; Reading Level: 2.5.

Little Otto, an alligator, and his animal friends set out to find the mischievous ghost pirate who has been disturbing the seaside village.

***Pie Rats Ahoy* by Richard Scarry** (New York: Random House, 1972); full-color illustrations; Interest Level: K-3; Reading Level: 1.9.

Uncle Willy takes a cruise on his boat and is overpowered by mice pirates until he develops a plan to outwit them.

***Pigs and Pirates: A Greek Tale* by Barbara Walker, illustrated by Harold Berson** (Lubbock, TX: David White 1969/1990); full-color illustrations; Interest and Reading Levels: not listed.

Three boys cleverly save their herd of pigs from a band of pirates.

***The Pirate Who Tried to Capture the Moon* by Dennis Haseley, illustrated by Sue Truesdell** (New York: HarperCollins Children's Books, 1983); yellow-wash illustrations; Interest Level: K-3; Reading Level: 3.7.

A crusty old pirate who tries to capture the moon is instead transformed by it.

***The Pirates of Bedford Street* by Rachel Isadora** (New York: Greenwillow Books, 1988); full-color illustrations; Interest Level: K-3; Reading Level: 2.8.

Inspired by an afternoon matinee, Joey recreates the story of Redbeard the Pirate using chalk on the sidewalk.

***The Trouble with Uncle* by Babette Cole** (Boston: Little, Brown & Co., 1992); full-color illustrations; Interest Level: K-3; Reading Level: 2.1.

Uncle, who happens to be a pirate, sets sail for adventure and, while he loses a treasure, returns with an unusual wife.

Nonfiction Resources

***From Gold to Money* by Ali Mitgutsch** (Minneapolis: Carolrhoda Books, 1984); full-color illustrations; Interest Level: K-3; Reading Level: 2.7.

The author explains how bartering progresses to trading with gold and how gold coins are created and stored.

***Happy Haunting: Halloween Costumes You Can Make* by Judith Conaway, illustrated by Renzo Barto** (Mahwah, NJ: Troll Associates, 1986); three-color illustrations; Interest Level: K-3; Reading Level: 3.3.

Contains simple instructions for 17 costume ideas including a pirate ghost, pirate tatoo, eye patch, and parrot puppet.

***The Pirate's Handbook* by Margarette Lincoln** (New York: Cobblehill Books, 1995); full-color illustrations and photographs; Interest and Reading Levels: not listed.

Contains a wealth of information about pirate customs, clothes, food, treasure maps, and lifestyles as well as craft ideas to turn the most hopeless "landlubber" into a fierce sea rover.

***Pirates: Robbers of the High Seas* by Gail Gibbons** (Boston: Little, Brown and Co., 1993); full-color illustrations; Interest Level: K-3; Reading Level: 4.9.

Traces the history of pirates, concentrating on the pirates of the Caribbean from the 1500s to the 1700s. The last three pages contain short biographies about the eight most famous pirates, plus legendary treasures that have not yet been found.

***Sunken Treasure* by Gail Gibbons** (New York: HarperCollins, 1988); full-color illustrations; Interest Level: K-3; Reading Level: 4.2.

True story of the search and rescue of the treasures from a Spanish galleon.

Recipe: Golden Coins

1 cup all-purpose flour, sifted

1/4 teaspoon salt

1 cup shredded cheddar cheese

1/2 cup (one stick) butter, softened but not melted

This recipe makes about 30 coins. Preheat oven to 350 degrees. Mix all four ingredients in a small bowl. (To decrease the mess, put the ingredients in a zip-locking plastic bag, squeeze out the air, and have the children knead the bag to mix the ingredients.) Roll into one-inch balls and place on an ungreased cookie sheet. Bake for 15 minutes.

Music Activity: "Pirate Song"

Use the accompanying actions as you sing this song.

PIRATE SONG (Sung to the tune "The Eensy Weensy Spider.")

The hairy, scary pirate climbed aboard my ship.   *(Pretend to climb.)*
He tore my sails and listened to them rip.   *(Pretend to rip fabric.)*
Then he climbed my mast and whacked it with a sword,   *(Pretend to brandish a sword.)*
So I grabbed him by his moustache and tossed him overboard.   *(Pretend to toss a large object.)*

Art Activity: Pirate Hat

Materials:

- black 18-inch by 12-inch construction paper (two sheets per child); safety scissors
- glue
- stapler
- photocopies of pirate symbols (one symbol per child)
- pirate hat pattern

Preparation:

Trace the pirate hat shape onto black construction paper, taking care to observe the fold line. Photocopy the pirate symbol.

Procedure:

Distribute the marked construction paper and pirate symbols. Have students cut out the hats and pirate symbol and glue a pirate symbol to the center of one of the hat shapes. Staple the sides of the hats together to fit the child's head.

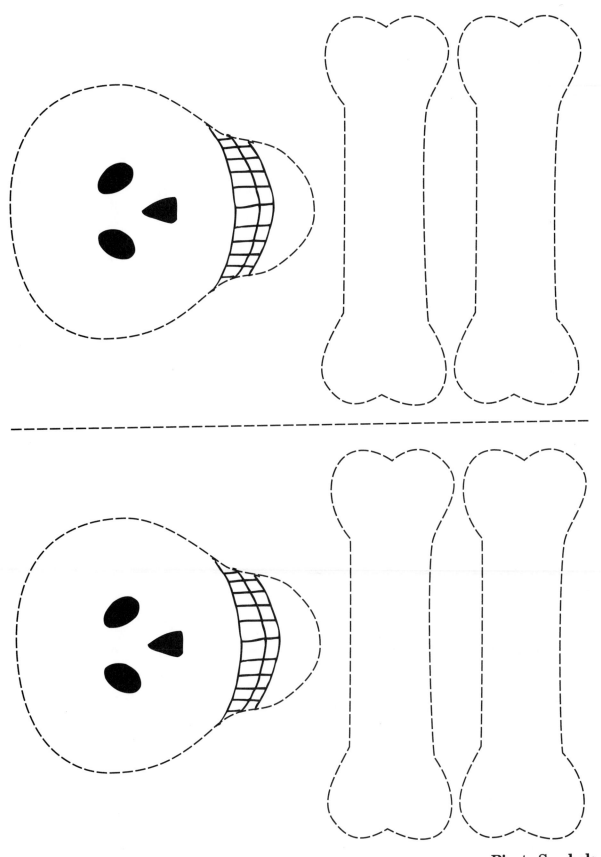

Pirate Symbols

Pirate Hat Pattern

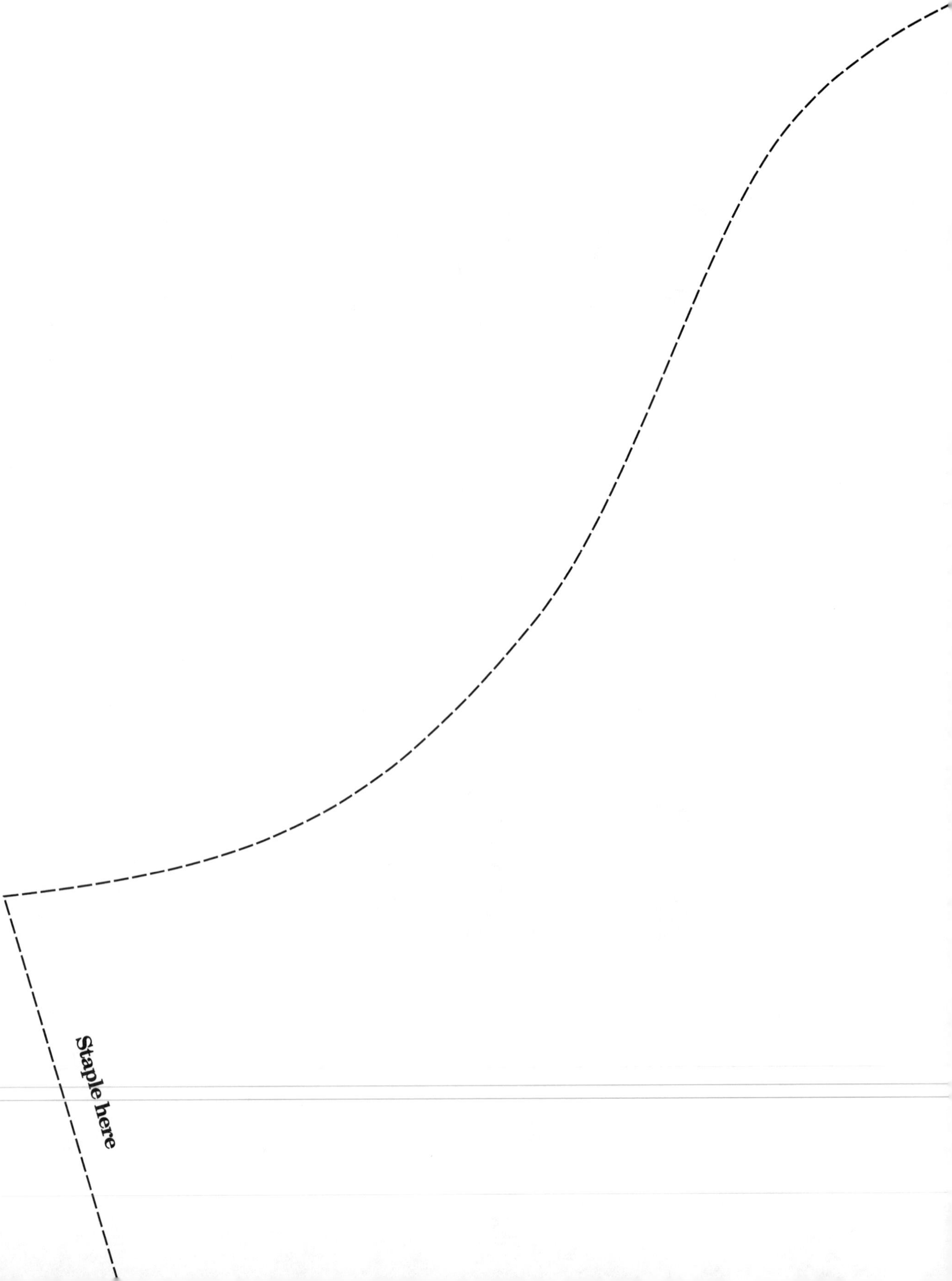

Staple here

Name _____ Date _____

Classroom Teacher _____

Pirates Research Project: Pirates of long ago sailed the Spanish Main searching for gold, jewelry, and coins. Coins are very interesting objects. A person who collects coins is called a numismatist.

Use a penny, a nickel, and a dime to answer the questions below.

PENNY: When was your penny minted? _____

What does the "heads" side of your penny say?

_____

What does the "tails" side of your penny say?

_____

NICKEL: When was your nickel minted? _____

_____

What does the "heads" side of your nickel say?

_____

What does the "tails" side of your nickel say?

_____

DIME: When was your dime minted? _____

What does the "heads" side of your dime say?

_____

What does the "tails" side of your dime say?

_____

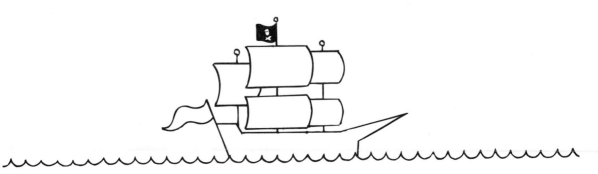

Quilt

Getting Ready to Teach the Letter Q

This unit lends itself to outside community resources. Perhaps a parent or grandparent would be willing to visit the library and demonstrate how a quilt is made. Or maybe community members would lend quilts to the library for a quilt show.

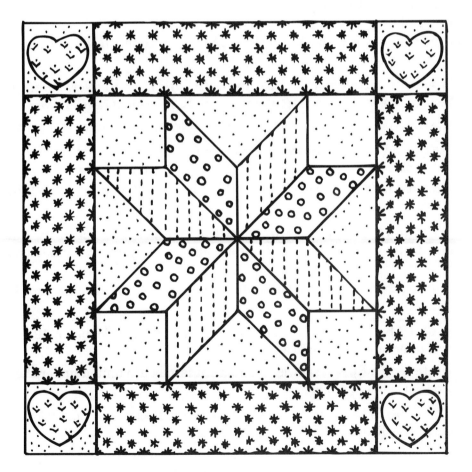

Objectives for Quilts:

Each child will be able to:

1. Match the letter "Q" with the word "quilt" and vice versa.

2. Summarize the read-aloud story in chronological order.

3. Identify the composition of a quilt and the procedure used to create a quilt.

Introductory Activity: A Needle and the Thread

Have students stand in a circle facing in. Explain and demonstrate how a needle and thread are used to quilt through two layers of fabric and batting. Choose one child to be the NEEDLE and another child, four spaces away, to be the THREAD. The rest of the children will be the FABRIC. Explain that when the leader says "Go," the NEEDLE will run in and out of the FABRIC—with the THREAD, also running in and out of the FABRIC, chasing him or her. The NEEDLE will try to return to his or her place without the THREAD catching him or her. When the first round is finished, choose two other children to repeat the process.

Recommended Books

***Bizzy Bones and the Lost Quilt* by Jacqueline Briggs Martin, illustrated by Stella Ormai** (New York: Lothrop, Lee & Shepard, 1988); full-color illustrations; Interest Level: K-3; Reading Level: 2.5.

Bizzy the mouse is devastated when he loses his beloved quilt. His friends help him find it and repair the damage.

***Ernest and Celestine's Patchwork Quilt* by Gabrielle Vincent** (New York: Greenwillow Books, 1982); full-color illustrations; Interest Level: K-3; Reading Level: no words.

Ernest and Celestine, a bear and a mouse, collect fabric samples and make a patchwork quilt.

***The Flying Patchwork Quilt* by Barbara Brenner, illustrated by Fred Brenner** (New York: Young Scott Books, 1965); two-color illustrations; Interest and Reading Levels: not listed.

A young girl pins an old quilt around her shoulders and finds that it magically transports her through town.

***My Mother's Patchwork Quilt: A Book and Pocketful of Patchwork Pieces* by Janet Bolton** (New York: Delacorte Press, 1993/94); full-color illustrations; Interest and Reading Levels: not listed.

Chronicles the patches on Grandmother's patchwork quilt. Contains materials and instructions to begin replicating the quilt.

***The Keeping Quilt* by Patricia Polacco** (New York: Simon & Schuster, 1988); full-color illustrations; Interest Level: K-3; Reading Level: 3.8.

Four generations of a Russian Jewish immigrant family are united under the traditions represented by a handmade quilt.

***Luka's Quilt* by Georgia Guback** (New York: Greenwillow Books, 1994); full-color illustrations; Interest Level: K-3; Reading Level: 2.3.

A young Hawaiian girl is disappointed with the traditional two-color quilt her grandmother makes for her until the grandmother finds a way to add colors to it without changing the tradition.

***The Quilt* by Ann Jonas** (New York: Puffin Books, 1984); full-color illustrations; Interest Level: K-3; Reading Level: 1.8.

A little girl goes to bed under her new quilt and dreams that her quilt has turned into a town.

***Quilts in the Attic* by Robbin Fleisher, pictures by Ati Forberg** (New York: Macmillan Publishing Co., 1978); full- and two-color illustrations; Interest Level: K-3; Reading Level: not listed.

Two sisters discover two quilts in the attic and use them to play sisterly games of imagination, competition, and love.

***Sewing Quilts* by Ann Turner, illustrated by Thomas B. Allen** (New York: Macmillan Publishing Co., 1994); full-color illustrations; Interest Level: K-3; Reading Level: 3.5.

A young pioneer girl helping her mother and sister sew a quilt recalls the events of her life.

***Sweet Clara and the Freedon Quilt* by Deborah Hopkinson, illustrated by James Ransome** (New York: Knopf/Random House, 1993); full-color illustrations; Interest Level: 3-6; Reading Level: 4.5.

A young girl, who is a slave in the South, sews a quilt, which actually is a map that guides her north to freedom.

Nonfiction Resources

***175 Easy-to-Do Christmas Crafts* edited by Sharon Dunn Umnik** (Honesdale, PA: Boyds Mills Press, 1996); full-color photographs; Interest and Reading Levels: not listed.

Contains directions for easy, kid-pleasing Christmas crafts. Projects include a quilted ornament, patchwork ornaments, and a Christmas card address book.

***Patchcraft: Designs, Material, Technique* by Elsie Svennas** (New York: Van Nostrand Reinhold Company, 1972); black-and-white photographs; Interest and Reading Levels: not listed.

Presents patchwork quilt projects parents could make for children including play tents, curtains, piggy banks, and wall hangings.

***Patchwork* by Judith Choate and Jane Green, illustrated by Carol Inouye** (New York: Doubleday & Co., 1976); two-color illustrations; Interest and Reading Levels: not listed.

Contains simple patchwork projects that young children, with extensive adult supervision, can complete. Projects include napkins, placemats, watchbands, clothing appliques, and pillows.

***Sewing by Hand* by Christine Hoffman, pictures by Harriet Barton** (New York: HarperCollins, 1994); full-color illustrations; Interest Level: 3-6; Reading Level: 4.9.

Contains directions to hand-sew a circle pillow, beanbag car, and a doll.

***Small Folk Quilters* by Ingrid Rogler** (Montrose, PA: Chitra Publications, 1989); black-and-white illustrations and color photographs; Interest and Reading Levels: not listed.

Presents step-by-step instructions for a small group or individual children to construct a quilt.

Recipe: Quilt Squares

1 loaf of sliced bread

1 cup milk

food coloring (red, blue, yellow, green)

Cut bread slices into equal squares. Pour 1/4 cup milk into 4 separate containers (such as cupcake tins). Put several drops of food coloring into the separate containers to create four paint colors. Using a small paintbrush, color each slice of bread. Toast the decorated bread in the toaster. Put the toasted bread together to make a quilt, then eat.

Music Activity: "The Quilt Song"

THE QUILT SONG (Sung to the tune "Round the Village.")

We'll   cut   and   sew   the   patch– es,   We'll

cut   and   sew   the   patch– es,   We'll   cut   and   sew   the

patch–   So   we   can   make   a   quilt.

Verse 1:   We'll cut and sew the patches,   *(Pretend to cut and hand-sew.)*
We'll cut and sew the patches,
We'll cut and sew the patches,
So we can make a quilt.

Verse 2:   We'll add the batting and backing,   *(Pretend to smooth batting and backing.)*
We'll add the batting and backing,
We'll add the batting and backing,
So we can make a quilt.

Verse 3:   We'll sew the layers together,   *(Pretend to hand-sew.)*
We'll sew the layers together,
We'll sew the layers together,
So we can make a quilt.

Verse 4:   We'll snuggle in our new quilt,   *(Pretend to drape a quilt around your*
We'll snuggle in our new quilt,   *shoulders.)*
We'll snuggle in our new quilt,
And we will go to sleep.   *(Pretend to fall asleep.)*

Art Activity: Quilt Square

Materials:

- wallpaper books (wallpaper stores may donate outdated wallpaper books to schools and libraries)
- safety scissors
- glue

Preparation:

Cut wallpaper samples into 6-inch squares. Give each child two squares.

Procedure:

Have each child choose two contrasting squares. The child is to use one square as the background and cut out and glue pieces of the other square onto the background. All of the squares can be assembled into a dramatic bulletin board.

Name _____

Date _____

Classroom Teacher _____

Rain Forest Research Project: Use a book that contains photographs of a variety of quilts to answer the questions below.

1. Do you see a quilt that contains square shapes?

   _____

2. Do you see a quilt that contains triangular shapes?

   _____

3. Do you see a quilt that contains rectangular shapes?

   _____

4. Do you see a quilt that contains circular shapes?

   _____

5. Do you see a quilt that contains oval shapes?

   _____

   Write the title of the book where you found your

   information: _____

Rain Forest

Getting Ready to Teach the Letter R

Create a rain forest environment by strewing rolls of green crepe paper on the bookshelves and from the ceiling. Replace overhead lights with green party light bulbs and play a rain forest audio tape. (*A Walk in the Rain Forest* [6DN 160C] is available from Educational Record Center, 3233 Burnt Mill Drive, Suite 100, Wilmington, North Carolina 28403-2655.)

Students also might want to bring in their stuffed animals to help decorate the forest. (See the invitation below.)

You may want to dress in khaki shorts, a bright T-shirt, hiking boots, and a pith helmet (available at Army/Navy surplus stores).

Dear Parents or Guardians,

We are planning to study rain forests within the next few days. We are creating a mock rain forest in the library and invite your child to add to the fun by bringing in a stuffed animal representing one or more of the following rain forest animals: bat, gibbon, monkey, squirrel, parrot, toucan, sloth, hummingbird, frog, lizard, snake, anteater, opposom, deer, hog, tapir, members of the cat family, ant, bee, butterfly, and spider.

Thank you for your continued support. Please feel free to call me if you have any questions or concerns.

Sincerely,

Objectives for Rain Forest:

Each child will be able to:

1. Match the letter "R" with the word "rain forest" and vice versa.

2. Summarize the read-aloud story in chronological order.

3. List the animals that live in a rain forest.

Introductory Activity: Anaconda Game

This game is best played in a marked-off area of the playground or in a gymnasium.

Explain to the class that anaconda snakes live in South American rain forests and that they may grow as long as 30 feet. Explain that the children will play a tag game called "Anaconda." One child will be named the ANACONDA and, when the game begins, will try to tag other classmates. When the ANACONDA tags another classmate, that child joins hands with the ANACONDA and together they try to tag additional children. The game ends when the last child is tagged.

Recommended Books

***Amazon Boy* written and illustrated by Ted Lewin** (New York: Macmillan Publishing Co., 1993); full-color illustrations; Interest Level: K-3; Reading Level: 4.5.

Paulo, to celebrate his birthday, travels from his Amazon River home to the bustling port of Belem. Slowly he realizes that the prosperity of the town is derived from the slow destruction of the Amazon rain forest.

***The Great Kapok Tree: A Tale of the Amazon Rain Forest* by Lynne Cherry** (San Diego: Harcourt Brace & Co., 1990); full-color illustrations; Interest Level: K-3; Reading Level: 4.4.

A man goes to the rain forest to fell a kapok tree until the animals that live in the tree convince him to leave it alone.

***Here Is the Tropical Rain Forest* by Madeleine Dunphy, illustrated by Michael Rothman** (Boston: Hyperion Books for Children, 1994); full-color illustrations; Interest Level: K-3; Reading Level: 4.9.

This cumulative free-verse poem describes the sights, sounds, flora, and fauna of a tropical rain forest. The end result is a vivid description of the forest's ecosystem.

***Jaguarundi* by Virginia Hamilton, paintings by Floyd Cooper** (New York: Scholastic, 1995); full-color illustrations.

A jaguarundi and coati must travel to a new land when men invade their rain forest and destroy their habitat.

***Jungle Days, Jungle Nights* by Martin and Tanis Jordan** (Las Vegas: Kingfisher Books, 1993); full-color photographs; Interest Level: 3-6; Reading Level: 5.8.

The author describes the many animals in a South American rain forest and their growth during a one-year period.

***Jungle Sounds* by Rebecca Emberly** (Boston: Little, Brown & Co., 1989); full-color illustrations; Interest Level: K-3; Reading Level: 1.5.

Contains large pictures of rain forest animals, the sounds they make, and their relationships within the ecosystem.

***Junglewalk* by Nancy Tafuri** (New York: Greenwillow Books, 1988); full-color illustrations; Interest Level: K-3; Reading Level: not listed.

After reading a book about jungles, a young boy dreams that his backyard is a jungle where he meets wild animals.

***Matepo* by Angela McAllister, illustrated by Jill Newton** (New York: Dial Books, 1991); full-color illustrations; Interest Level: K-3; Reading Level: 5.3.

Matepo the monkey wants to take fruit to his mother. By trading and bartering with the other jungle animals, he finally accomplishes his goal.

***The Rain Forest* created by Gallimard Jeunesse and Rene' Mettler, illustrated by Rene' Mettler** (New York: Scholastic, 1992/1994); full-color illustrations; Interest Level: K-3; Reading Level: not listed.

Transparent overlays and vivid illustrations demonstrate the flora and fauna that live in a rain forest.

***Ten Sly Piranyas: A Counting Story in Reverse* by William Wise, illustrated by Victoria Chess** (New York: Dial Books for Young Readers, 1993); full-color illustrations; Interest Level: K-3; Reading Level: 4.5.

Ten humorous piranhas teach reverse counting from ten to zero by eating each other.

***Who Is the Beast?* written and illustrated by Keith Baker** (San Diego: Harcourt Brace Jovanovich, 1990); full-color illustrations; Interest Level: K-3; Reading Level: 1.7.

Animals in an Indian jungle flee from the sight of a tiger until the tiger points out his similarities with the other jungle animals.

Nonfiction Resources

***Amazing Tropical Birds: Eyewitness Juniors* by Gerald Legg, photographs by Jerry Young** (New York: Alfred A. Knopf, 1991); full-color photographs and illustrations; Interest Level: K-3; Reading Level: 5.3.

Contains pictures of beautiful and exotic birds and explanations of their appearance and physical features.

***Animals of the Tropics* adapted by Cathy Poth from an original French text by Pierre Averous, illustrated by Isabelle Molinard** (Parsippany, NJ: Silver Burdett Press, 1989); full-color illustrations; Interest Level: 3-6; Reading Level: 4.8.

Contains a large ecoland illustration and, on the following pages, identifications and descriptions of each wildlife creature in the illustration.

***At Home in the Rain Forest* by Diane Willow, illustrated by Laura Jacques** (Watertown, MA: Charlesbridge, 1991); full-color illustrations; Interest Level: 3-6; Reading Level: 6.1.

Illustrations and text introduce readers to the flora and fauna in the Amazon rain forest.

***Discover Rain Forests* by Lynne Hardie Baptista, consultant Richard Block** (Lincolnwood, IL: Publications International, 1992); full-color illustrations; Interest and Reading Levels: not listed.

Contains both simple and advanced explanations about the beautiful and unusual sights in a rain forest.

***The Rain Forest* by Billy Goodman** (Mankato, MN: Creative Education, 1991); full-color illustrations; Interest Level: 3-6; Reading Level: 6.7.

Presents fascinating information of the rain forest and the creatures that inhabit it.

Recipe: Sunrise on the Amazon

3 cups water

1 12-ounce container lemonade concentrate

3 drops yellow food coloring

32 ounces prepared orange juice, chilled

1 liter ginger ale, chilled

1 12-ounce container grenadine syrup

optional: fresh tropical fruit

This recipe makes about 8 servings. Prepare lemonade concentrate according to directions on the label. Add food coloring and pour mixture into ice cube trays and freeze. When frozen, crush ice. Place about 1/2 cup crushed lemonade into clear plastic 7-ounce cups. Pour 1/4 cup each orange juice and ginger ale over the ice. Slowly pour 1 tablespoon grenadine syrup into the middle of each drink. Serve without stirring.

Optional: Garnish drink with fresh fruit, cut into bite-size pieces, and skewer on a plastic coffee stir stick.

Music Activity: "A Monkey in a Great Kapok Tree"

Refer to the accompanying illustrations and finger plays.

A MONKEY IN A GREAT KAPOK TREE
(Sung to the tune "The Twelve Days of Christmas.")

rain for—est and   what do you think we   see?

Four an—a—con—da, three but—ter—flies,   two   fly— ing

squir—rels, and a   mon—key in a   great ka—   pok

tree.   We   walk—ing   in   the

rain   for—est and   what do you think we   see?

Five   black   ta—   ran—tu—las,

four   an—a—con—da, three but—ter—flies,   two   fly—   ing

squir—rels, and a   mon—key in a   great ka—   pok

tree.   We   walk—ing   in   the

rain   for—est and   what do you think we   see?

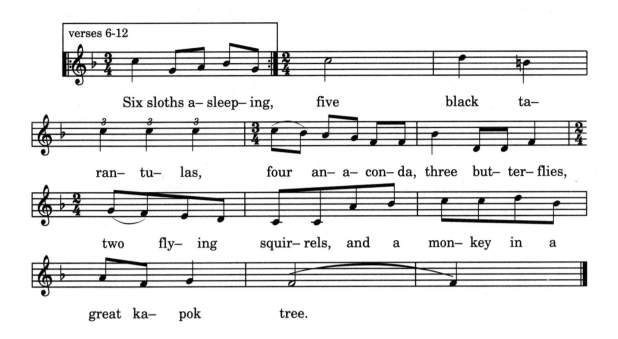

Six sloths a– sleep– ing,   five   black   ta–

ran– tu– las,   four an– a– con– da, three but– ter– flies,

two   fly– ing   squir– rels, and   a   mon– key   in   a

great ka– pok   tree.

7. seven ants a-marching

8. eight toucans squawking

9. nine frogs a-hopping

10. ten hummingbirds a-fluttering

11. eleven jaguars stalking

12. twelve anteaters eating

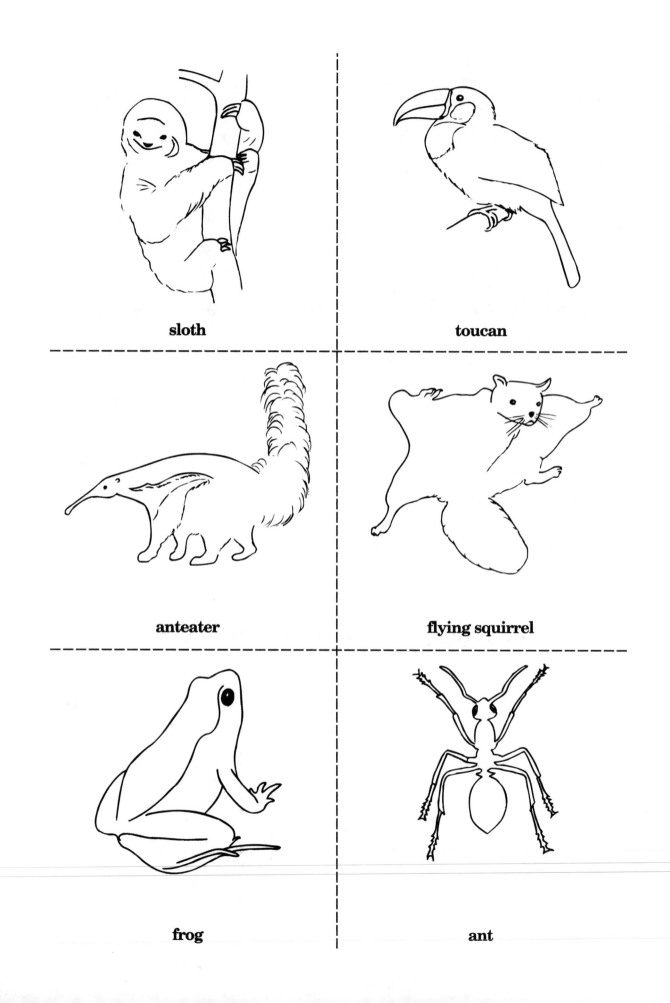

sloth

toucan

anteater

flying squirrel

frog

ant

kapok tree

hummingbird

anaconda

butterfly

tarantula

jaguar

Finger Play Verses with Movements

Verse 1:   We are walking   *(Walk in place.)*

                In the rain forest   *(Run hands from head to waist, moving fingers rapidly up and down.)*

                And what do you think we see?   *(Hold side of right hand to right eyebrow as if saluting.)*

                A monkey   *(Place hands under arms.)*

                In a great kapok tree.   *(Place arms straight above head and move arms downward, creating a large arc.)*

Verse 2:   Two flying squirrels   *(Place arms out from the side of the body as if gliding through the air.)*

Verse 3:   Three butterflies   *(Hook thumbs together and move the hands up and down in unison.)*

Verse 4:   Four anacondas   *(Place palms together in front of body and move hands, in a swaying motion, left to right.)*

Verse 5:   Five black tarantulas   *(Hold one hand out, palm face up. Place fingers of the other hand on the palm to resemble a spider.)*

Verse 6:   Six sloths a-sleeping   *(Tip head to the right, close eyes and place hands, palms together, on the right temple.)*

Verse 7:   Seven ants a-marching   *(March in place.)*

Verse 8:   Eight toucans squawking   *(Hook thumbs under arms and flap elbows.)*

Verse 9:   Nine frogs a-hopping   *(Hop in place.)*

Verse 10:   Ten hummingbirds a-fluttering   *(Flap arms rapidly.)*

Verse 11:   Eleven jaguars stalking   *(Move hands in a circular motion in front of body to resemble the front legs of a jaguar when it is walking.)*

Verse 12:   Twelve anteaters eating.   *(Lick lips and rub tummy.)*

Art Activity: Rain Forest Straw Sippers

Materials:

- photocopies of the straw sippers patterns (one page serves two students)
- crayons
- straws (one per child)
- safety scissors
- X-acto™ knife

Preparation:

Photocopy the straw sipper page and cut in half as indicated. Use an X-acto™ knife to cut two slits, as marked, in each straw slipper.

Procedure:

Have students color and cut out the straw sippers. Use the slits to fit a straw through the sippers. The sippers can be used to drink the "Amazon Sunrise" recipe.

Straw Sippers Patterns

Name _____ Date _____

Classroom Teacher _____

Rain Forest Research Project: Tropical rain forests are home to many varieties of monkeys including the proboscis monkey. Find a picture of a proboscis monkey by looking up "monkey" or "proboscis monkey" in an encyclopedia or other reference source. Finish drawing the nose of the proboscis monkey below.

Write the title of the book where you found your information:

_____

_____

_____

Spaghetti

Getting Ready to Teach the Letter S

Spaghetti was developed in Italy in the 1200s. With this in mind, dress as an Italian chef with an apron and chef's hat. Also carry a mixing bowl and wooden spoon, and play an audio tape of Italian music (available from LDMI, P.O. Box 1445, St. Laurent, Quebec, Canada H4L 4Z1).

Bring a tree or potted branch to class. Before class begins, string 8-inch lengths of off-white yarn on the tree and hang tiny brown balls, made of clay, from the branches. Explain, tongue-in-cheek, that the plant is a spaghetti tree and that in the spring the tiny balls grow into meatballs. You pluck the spaghetti and meatballs from the tree to prepare dinner. Ask students to raise their hands if they believe you. When no one raises a hand, discuss how spaghetti is really made! This discussion includes a sample of uncooked spaghetti and, if possible, a pasta machine.

Objectives for Spaghetti:

Each child will be able to:

1. Match the letter "S" with the word "spaghetti" and vice versa.

2. Summarize the read-aloud story in chronological order.

3. Briefly describe the origin of spaghetti and explain how spaghetti is prepared.

Introductory Activity: Spaghetti Tangle Game

Choose one child to be the "meatball." The other children line up, all facing in the same direction, and hold hands. This line of children represents a "strand of spaghetti." When the "meatball" leaves the room, the children are to tangle themselves while continuing to hold hands. The children may go under or over other children, with the supervision of the teacher. The "meatball" is called back and must try to untangle the children, who continue to hold hands, and recreate a straight line again.

Recommended Books

***Daddy Makes the Best Spaghetti* by Anna Grossnickle Hines** (New York: Clarion Books, 1986); full-color illustrations; Interest Level: K-3; Reading Level: 2.5.

Daddy picks up Corey at the day care center and together they go home, prepare a spaghetti dinner, and get ready for bed.

***Freddie's Spaghetti* by Charlotte Doyle, illustrated by Nicholas Reilly** (New York: Random House, 1991); full-color illustrations; Interest Level: K-3; Reading Level: 1.5.

Freddie must learn patience as his mother prepares spaghetti for dinner.

***More Spaghetti, I Say!* by Rita Gordon Gelman, illustrated by Mort Gerberg** (New York: Scholastic, text 1977, illustrations 1992; full-color illustrations; Interest Level: K-3; Reading Level: 1.0.

A monkey named Minnie will not play with his best friend, Freddie, because Minnie is eating and playing in vast quantities of spaghetti.

***One Saturday Morning* by Barbara Baker, illustrated by Kate Duke** (New York: Dutton Children's Books, 1994); full-color illustrations; Interest Level: K-3; Reading Level: 1.7.

A family enjoys a Saturday morning together, waking up, going to the park, and eating spaghetti for lunch.

***Peanut Butter, Apple Butter, Cinnamon Toast: Food Riddles for You to Guess* by Argentina Palacios** (Chatham, NJ: Raintree, 1990); full-color illustrations; Interest Level: K-3; Reading Level: 2.1.

Rhyming riddles describe various foods including spaghetti.

***Spaghetti for Suzy* by Peta Coplans** (Boston: Houghton Mifflin, 1993); full-color illustrations; Interest Level: K-3; Reading Level: 1.8.

A young girl tries to eat other foods but decides that spaghetti still is her favorite.

***The Spaghetti Party* by Doris Orgel, illustrated by Julie Durrell** (New York: Bantam Books, 1995); full-color illustrations; Interest Level: K-3; Reading Level: 2.5.

Annie and her friends enjoy a come-as-you-are spaghetti party.

***The Stories Huey Tells* by Ann Cameron, illustrated by Roberta Smith** (New York: Knopf, 1995); illustrations; Interest Level: K-3; Reading Level: 2.8.

Huey experiences many adventures including his invention of banana spaghetti.

***Strega Nona* written and illustrated by Tomie dePaola** (New York: Simon and Schuster Books for Young Children, 1975); full-color illustrations; Interest Level: K-3; Reading Level: 4.4.

Strega Nona, who possesses special powers, makes magic pots of spaghetti. Big Anthony overhears her magic chants and tries to duplicate her magic, but instead creates a gigantic mess.

***Wednesday Is Spaghetti Day* written and illustrated by Maryann Cocca Leffler** (New York: Scholastic, 1990); full-color illustrations; Interest Level: K-3; Reading Level: 1.9.

When the family leaves the house, the cat, Catrina, invites her cat friends to the house for an uproarious spaghetti lunch.

Nonfiction Resources

***Count Your Way Through Italy* by James Haskins, illustrated by Beth Wright** (Minneapolis: Carolrhoda Books, 1990); full-color illustrations; Interest Level: K-3; Reading Level: 4.2.

The book introduces the numbers one to ten in Italian through a tour of Italian culture.

***Italy* by Donna Bailey and Anna Sproule** (New York: Steck-Vaughn, 1990); full-color illustrations; Interest Level: K-3; Reading Level: 2.4.

Text and illustrations show the beauty and people of Italy.

***Pasta Factory* by Hana Machotka** (Boston: Houghton Mifflin, 1992); full-color photographs; Interest Level: 3-6; Reading Level: 5.3.

A group of children tour the Tutta Pasta factory to learn how different types of pasta, as well as tomato sauce, are made.

***Siggy's Spaghetti Works* by Peggy Thomson, illustrated by Gloria Kamen** (New York: Tambourine Books, 1993); full-color illustrations; Interest Level: K-3; Reading Level: 3.9.

A cook named Siggy gives a tour of his factory to young children to demonstrate a pasta-making machine. Includes pictures and text about the origin of pasta.

***A Taste of Italy* by Jenny Ridgwell** (New York: Thomson Learning, 1993); full-color illustrations; Interest Level: 3-6; Reading Level: 4.9.

Presents the origin and uses of traditional Italian food including pasta, meat, fish, and cheese. Includes recipes and a glossary.

Recipe: Spaghetti-Tasting Party

1 16-ounce box of spaghetti

1 14-ounce bottle commercially prepared spaghetti sauce

3 different pasta sauce flavor packets*

necessary ingredients per the directions on the
pasta sauce packets

Prepare the spaghetti according to the directions on the box. Heat the spaghetti sauce. Prepare the pasta sauces according to the directions on the packages. Place several small mounds of spaghetti on each child's plate and put a different pasta sauce on each mound. Have children sample the various flavors and decide which is his or her favorite.

Extension: Create a bar graph to demonstrate the popularity of each sauce.

*Pasta sauce packets are available at most grocery stores. Two suppliers are: Knorr, c/o CPC Specialty Markets U.S.A., Indianapolis, Indiana 46221-1070, and Spice Islands Pasta Gourmet, A Division of Burns Philip Food Inc., San Francisco, CA 94108.

Music Activity: "Meatball Counting Song"

See the accompanying finger plays for this song. For more fun, use the meatball puppet made in the Art Activity in conjunction with the finger plays.

MEATBALL COUNTING SONG (Sung to the tune "Ten Little Indians.")

Verse 1: Uno (OO-noh) little due (DOO-eh) little tre (treh) little meatballs, Quattro (KWAHT-troh) little cinque (CHEEN-kweh) little sei (SEH-ee) little meatballs, Sette (SEHT-tay) little otto (OT-toh) little nove (NO-vah) little meatballs, Dieci (dee-AY-chee) little meatballs on my plate.

(Hold out two clenched fists and uncurl one finger for each number as it is sung.)

(Hold open hands together, palms up, to resemble a plate.)

Verse 2: Dieci (dee-AY-chee) little nove (NO-vah) little otto (OT-toh) little meatballs, Sette (SEHT-tay) little sei (SEH-ee) little cinque (CHEEN-kweh) little meatballs, Quattro (KWAHT-troh) little tre (treh) little due (DOO-eh) little meatballs, Uno (OO-noh) little meatballs in my tummy.

(Curl each finger into a clenched fist for each number as it is sung.)

(Rub tummy.)

Art Activity: Meatball Finger Puppet

Materials:
- disposable plastic gloves* (two per child)
- crayons
- safety scissors
- glue
- photocopies of the meatball patterns (1/2 sheet or ten meatballs per child)
- off-white yarn cut into 4-inch lengths (6 lengths per child)

Preparation:

Photocopy the meatballs and cut the pages in half along the dotted line down the center of the paper. Cut the yarn into 4-inch lengths.

Procedure:

Have students color, cut out, and glue the meatballs to the tips of the glove fingertips, one meatball per finger. Glue the lengths of yarn onto the gloves to resemble spaghetti. These puppets can be used to sing the "Meatball Counting Song" from the Music Activity.

*These gloves are available at variety, discount department, hardware, and food preparation stores. In addition, the school cafeteria personnel may be able to give or sell you a sufficient quantity of gloves for your children.

Meatball Patterns

Name _____ Date _____

Classroom Teacher _____

Spaghetti Research Project: Spaghetti was invented in Italy. Use an atlas or other reference source to locate a map of Italy. Locate and label the following Italian cities on the map below: Rome, Florence, and Venice.

Write the name of the reference source where you found your information:

_____

_____

Turtles and Tortoises

Getting Ready to Teach the Letter T

Before class begins, cut varying lengths of yarn and place the lengths on the floor between the library entrance door and the children's seats. When the children are at the door to enter the library, ask them to imagine they are turtle hatchlings and that the yarn pieces on the floor represent snakes—turtles' natural enemy. Challenge the children to slowly walk to their seats without stepping on any snakes.

Objectives for Turtles and Tortoises:

Each child will be able to:

1. Match the letter "T" with the word "turtle" and vice versa.

2. Summarize the read-aloud story in chronological order.

3. List the physical characteristics of turtles and describe their environments.

Introductory Activity: Turtle Cutting Story

Materials:

- six paper fasteners
- one photocopy of the turtle appendages patterns
- crayons
- scissors
- one 9-inch paper plate
- paper punch

Preparation:

Color the paper plate to resemble a turtle shell. Color and cut out the turtle legs, tail, and head. Use a paper punch to create holes in the shell and, where indicated, in the legs, tail, and head.

Procedure:

Beginning with the left front leg and proceeding counterclockwise, read an interesting fact about turtles as listed on each turtle part. After reading each fact, use a paper fastener to join that turtle part with the paper plate shell. The last fact should be the one listed on the head. As you read that fact, turn the legs, head, and tail inward, revealing only the turtle shell.

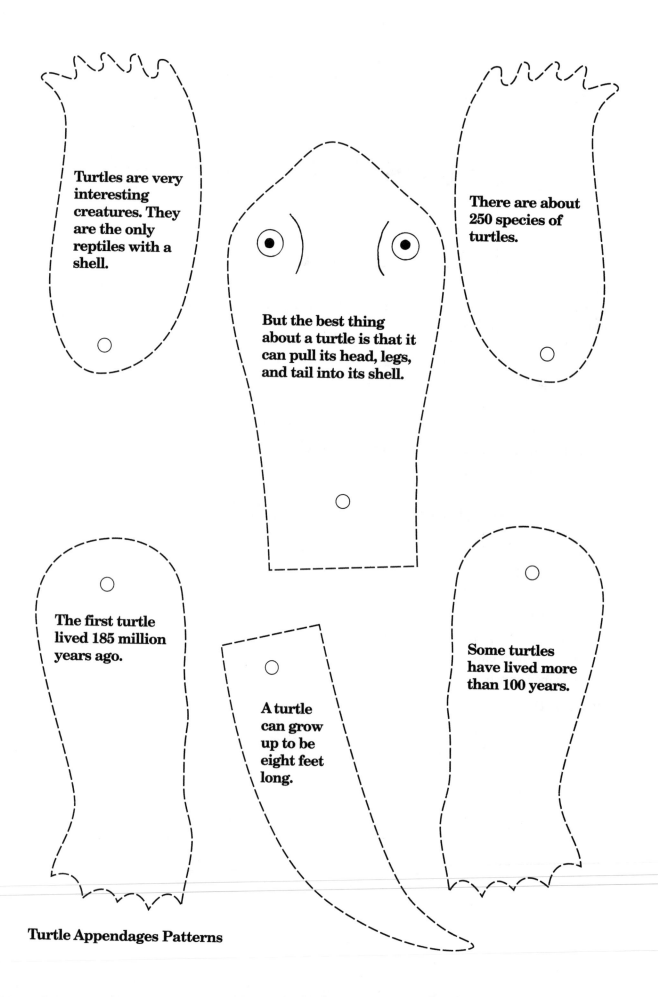

Turtles are very interesting creatures. They are the only reptiles with a shell.

There are about 250 species of turtles.

But the best thing about a turtle is that it can pull its head, legs, and tail into its shell.

The first turtle lived 185 million years ago.

A turtle can grow up to be eight feet long.

Some turtles have lived more than 100 years.

Turtle Appendages Patterns

Recommended Books

***Box Turtle at Long Pond* by William T. George, illustrated by Lindsay Barrett George** (New York: Greenwillow Books, 1989); full-color illustrations; Interest Level: K-3; Reading Level: 2.5.

The realistic text and illustrations describe a day in the life of a box turtle in the autumn.

***Franklin books* by Paulette Bourgeois, illustrated by Brenda Clark** (New York: Scholastic; full-color illustrations; Interest Level: K-3; Reading Level: about 2.3.
Titles include:
Franklin Fibs
Franklin in the Dark
Franklin Is Bossy
Franklin Is Lost
Hurry Up, Franklin

***The Hare and the Tortoise* retold by Caroline Castle, illustrated by Peter Weevers** (New York: Dial Books, 1985); full-color illustrations; Interest Level: K-3; Reading Level: 3.4.

This lively retelling of Aesop's classic tale recounts the race between a slow but consistent turtle and a quick but overly-confident hare.

***I Can't Get My Turtle to Move* by Elizabeth Lee O'Donnell, illustrations by Maxie Chambliss** (New York: Morrow Junior Books, 1989); full-color illustrations; Interest Level: K-3; Reading Level: 1.9.

In this counting book, a little girl finally gets her turtle to move by offering it lunch.

***Let's Get Turtles* by Millicent E. Selsam, illustrated by Arnold Lobel** (New York: Harper & Row, 1965); two-color illustrations; Interest and Reading Levels: not listed.

Two friends each get a turtle from the pet shop and work hard to properly care for them.

***Old Turtle's Riddle and Joke Book* by Leonard Kessler** (New York: Greenwillow Books, 1986); two-color illustrations; Interest Level: K-3; Reading Level: 2.2.

Old Turtle, with the help of his friends, writes a book of riddles—which are included in this book.

***The Tortoise and the Hare (An Aesop Fable)* adapted and illustrated by Janet Stevens** (New York: Holiday House, 1984); full-color illustrations; Interest Level: K-3; Reading Level: 3.0.

The classic tale of a slow and steady tortoise beating a quick but inconsistent rabbit is told with humor in a modern setting.

***Tricky Tortoise* by Mwenye Hadithi, illustrated by Adrienne Kennaway** (Boston: Little, Brown & Co., 1988); full-color illustrations; Interest Level: K-3; Reading Level: 2.5.

Tortoise develops a plan to stop Elephant from constantly stepping on his shell.

***Turtle Day* by Douglas Florian** (New York: Thomas Y. Crowell, 1989); full-color illustrations; Interest Level: K-3; Reading Level: 2.0.

Turtle spends an adventurous day at a pond.

***Turtle's Shell* written and illustrated by Sal Murdocca** (New York: Lothrop, Lee & Shepard, 1976); brown-and-orange illustrations; Interest Level: K-3; Reading Level: 2.8.

Tuttle the Turtle loses his shell and enlists his friends to help him retrieve it.

Nonfiction Resources

***Explore a Spooky Swamp* by Wendi Cortesi, photographs by Joseph H. Bailey** (Washington, DC: National Geographic Society, 1978); full-color photographs; Interest and Reading Levels: not listed.

Two children explore the many creatures in Okefenokee Swamp with an adult guide.

***Look Out for Turtles* by Melvin Berger, illustrated by Megan Lloyd** (New York: HarperCollins, 1992); full-color illustrations; Interest Level: K-3; Reading Level: 3.5.

Describes the variety, life cycle, habits, and habitats of turtles.

***Turtle and Tortoise* by Vincent Serventy** (New York: Raintree Children's Books, 1985); full-color photographs; Interest Level: K-3; Reading Level: 3.2.

Contains information about the life cycle, habitats, and variety of turtles and tortoises.

***The Turtle Book* by Mel Crawford** (New York: Golden Press Book, 1965); full-color illustrations; Interest Level: K-3; Reading Level: 2.4.

Brief text and large, colorful illustrations document the activities of a turtle at a pond.

***Turtles* by The Cousteau Society** (New York: Little Simon, 1992); full-color photographs; Interest and Reading Levels: not listed.

Contains information about green turtles.

***Turtles, Toads & Frogs* by George S. Fichter, illustrated by Barbara Hoopes Ambler** (New York: Golden Books, 1993); full-color illustrations; Interest Level: K-3; Reading Level: 4.9.

Text and realistic illustrations describe many species of turtles.

Recipe: Peanut Butter Turtles

1/2 cup honey

1 cup peanut butter

1 cup nonfat powdered milk

1-1/2 cups graham cracker crumbs

1 package mini-chocolate chips

This recipe makes about 12 turtles. Combine the honey, peanut butter, powdered milk, and cracker crumbs. Knead to form a ball. For each turtle, roll one 1-inch ball, one 3/4-inch ball, and five 1/2-inch balls. Form the 1-inch ball into a 2-inch patty. Use the patty as the turtle body, the medium ball as the head, and the small balls as the legs and tail. Squeeze the balls together to form a turtle. Place two mini-chocolate chips on the head to serve as eyes and press additional chips on the body to serve as the shell. Refrigerate one hour or more to harden slightly. Serve with milk.

Music Activity: "The Turtle Game"

Before class begins, use the pattern to create a felt turtle. When class begins, have students stand in a circle, holding hands and facing inward. Choose one child to be IT. Have that child stand outside the circle holding the felt turtle. Have students continuously sing the song while IT walks around the circle. At any point in the song, IT may drop the felt turtle behind one of the children and begin to run around the circle to the chosen child's spot. In the meantime, the chosen child is to pick up the turtle and, running in the same direction as IT, try to tag IT before he or she reaches the child's spot. The chosen child then becomes IT and the game continues as before.

THE TURTLE GAME (Sung to the tune "Row, Row, Row Your Boat.")

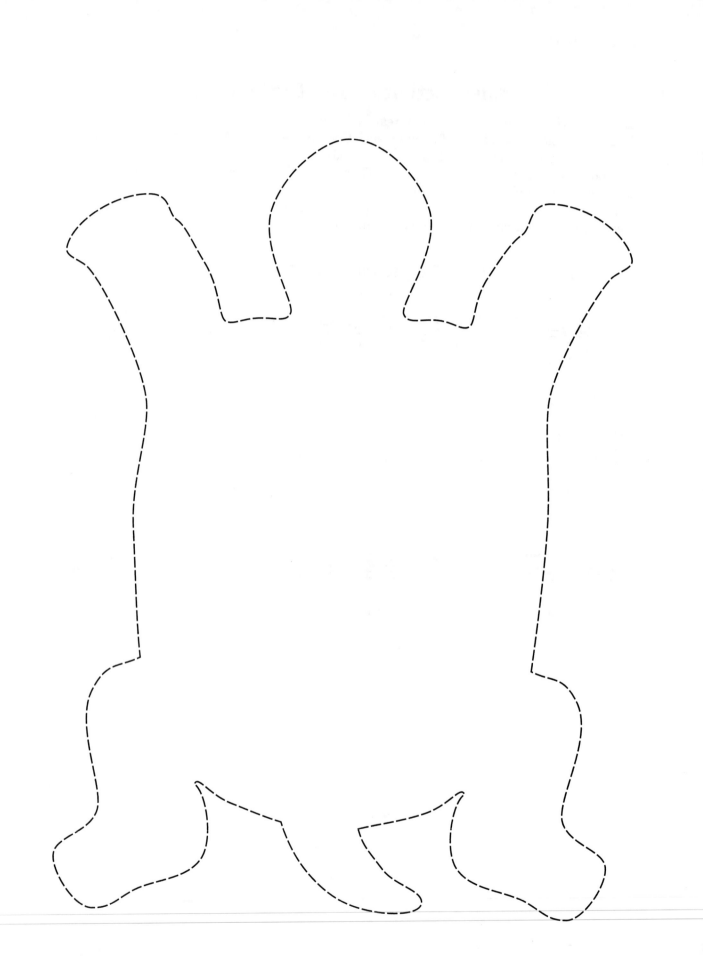

Turtle Pattern

Art Activity: Turtles

Materials:

- paper plates (one per child)
- paper fasteners (six per child)
- paper punch
- crayons
- safety scissors
- turtle parts patterns

Preparation:

Photocopy the turtle parts patterns. Use a paper punch to create holes in the paper plate where the turtle legs, head, and tail will be joined to the paper plate.

Procedure:

Have students color and cut out the turtle legs, head, and tail. Have students use the paper punch to create a hole, where indicated, on the legs, head, and tail. Direct children to color the paper plate to represent the turtle shell. Use paper fasteners to join the turtle parts to the paper plate. Show children how to retract the legs, tail, and head into the turtle shell.

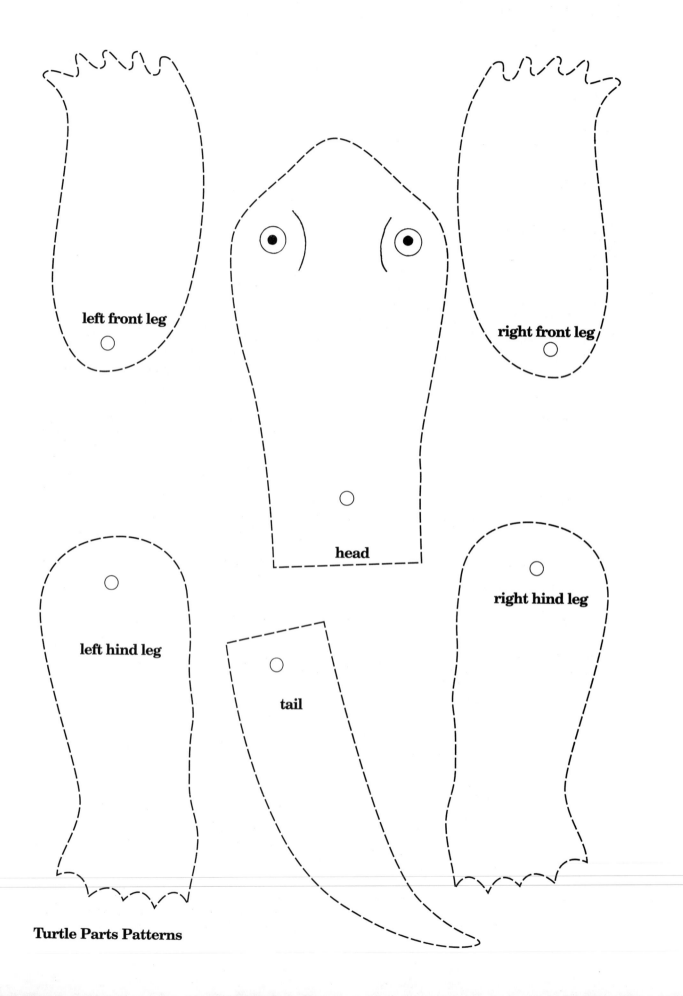

left front leg

right front leg

head

left hind leg

right hind leg

tail

Turtle Parts Patterns

Name _____ Date _____

Classroom Teacher _____

Turtles and Tortoises Research Project: A turtle is a member of the reptile family. Look up "reptile" in an encyclopedia or other reference source. Name four other members of the reptile family on the lines below.

_____

_____

_____

_____

Draw a picture of a reptile in the space below.

Write the title of the book where you found your information:

_____

The fastest reptile is the Pacific leatherback turtle which can swim up to 22 miles per hour.

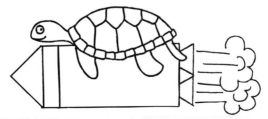

Undersea World

Getting Ready to Teach the Letter U

Set the stage for this unit by switching regular white light bulbs to blue and green light bulbs. Also hang green crepe paper streamers to represent seaweed, and construction paper fish from the ceiling. For added effect, Ocean Sounds audiotape 6DN 170 is available from Educational Record Center, 3233 Burnt Mill Drive, Suite 100, Wilmington, North Carolina 28403-2655 (1-800-438-1637).

Objectives of Undersea World:

Each child will be able to:

1. Match the letter "U" with the word "undersea" and vice versa.

2. Summarize the read-aloud story in chronological order.

3. Name a variety of animals that live in the ocean.

Introductory Activity: Marine Biologists' Game

Materials:

- photocopies of patterns of undersea creatures
- crayons
- scissors
- large blue tablecloth or sheet
- tape
- thick dowel rod
- large paper clips
- 36-inch length of string or yarn
- magnet
- penny toys and/or wrapped candy

Preparation:

Photocopy, color, and cut out the undersea creatures patterns. There should be one underwater sea creature per child. Place a large paper clip near the mouth of each creature. Spread out a tablecloth or sheet on the floor of the library to represent the ocean. Spread the undersea creatures on the sheet or tablecloth. Construct a fishing rod by tying a length of string or yarn to a dowel rod. Tape or tie a magnet to the end of the string to serve as a hook. Also tape a small penny toy or piece of wrapped candy to each creature.

Procedure:

Have students stand around the sheet. Point out and name the creatures in the "ocean." Explain that the children are marine biologists and they are to use the fishing pole to "catch" a sea creature, identify it, and put it back in the ocean. If the child can correctly name the creature, he or she may keep the prize taped to it. Give the fishing pole to one of the children and begin the game, continuing until all students have had an opportunity to go fishing.

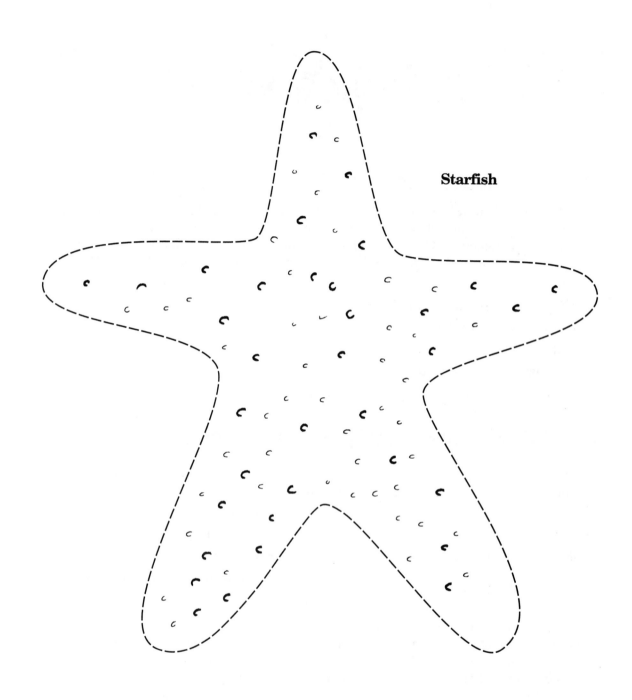

Starfish

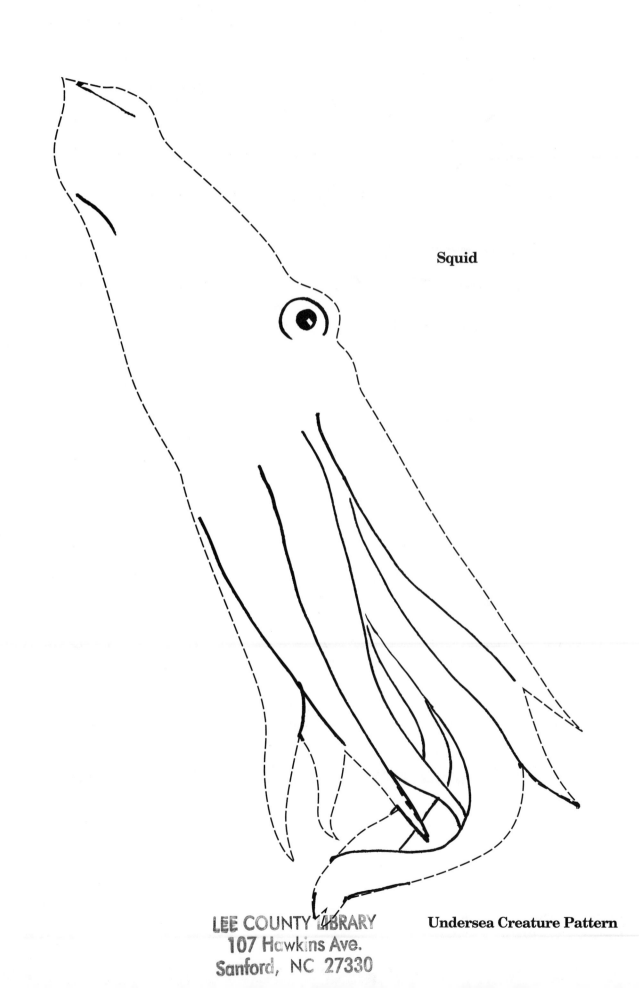

Squid

Undersea Creature Pattern

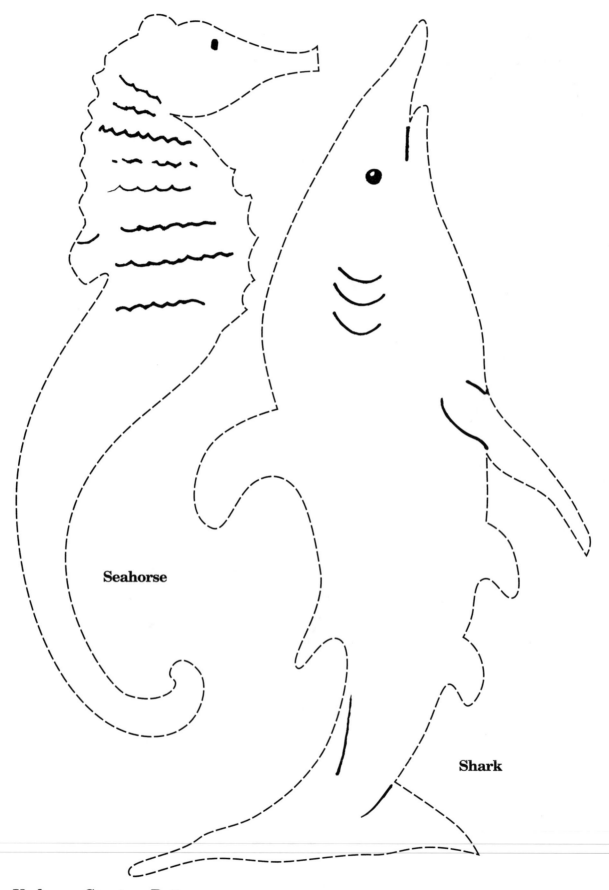

Seahorse

Shark

Undersea Creature Patterns

Crab

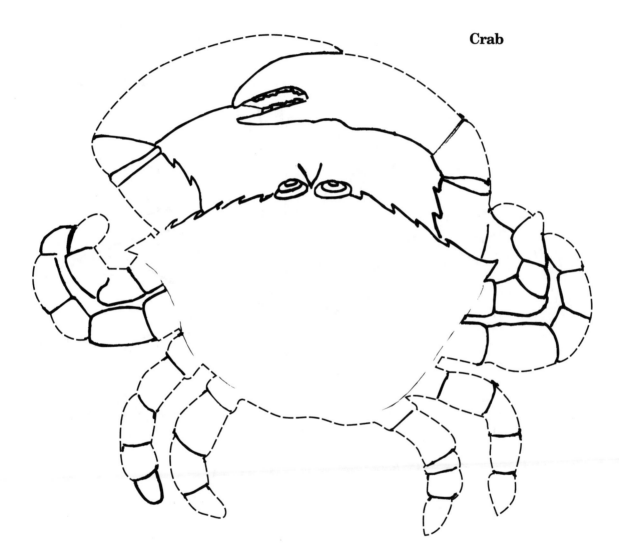

Undersea Creature Pattern

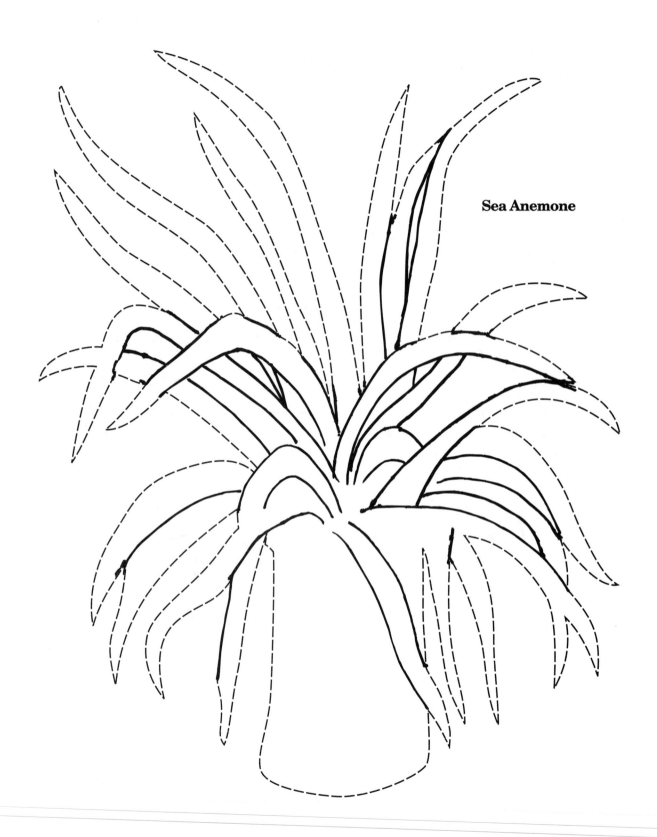

Sea Anemone

Undersea Creature Pattern

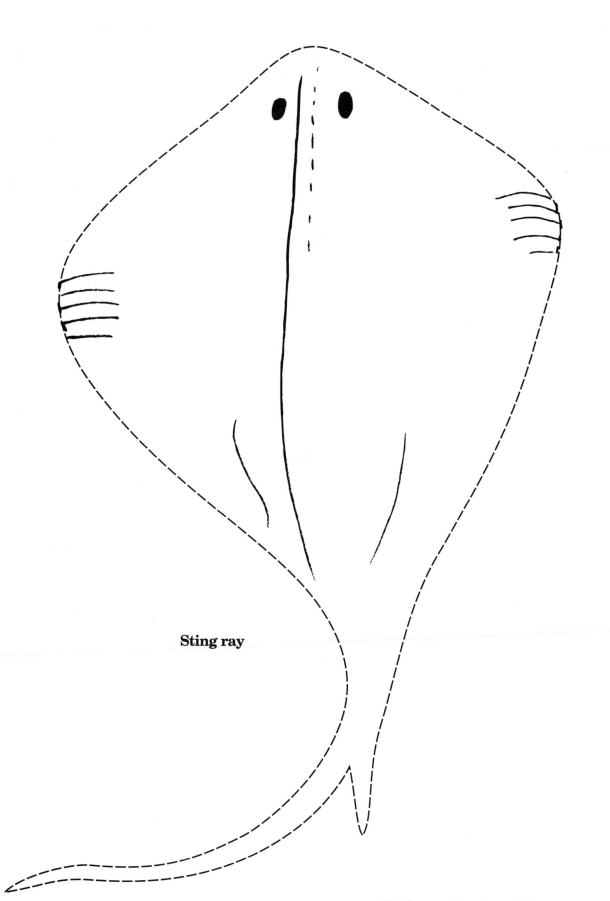

Sting ray

Undersea Creature Pattern

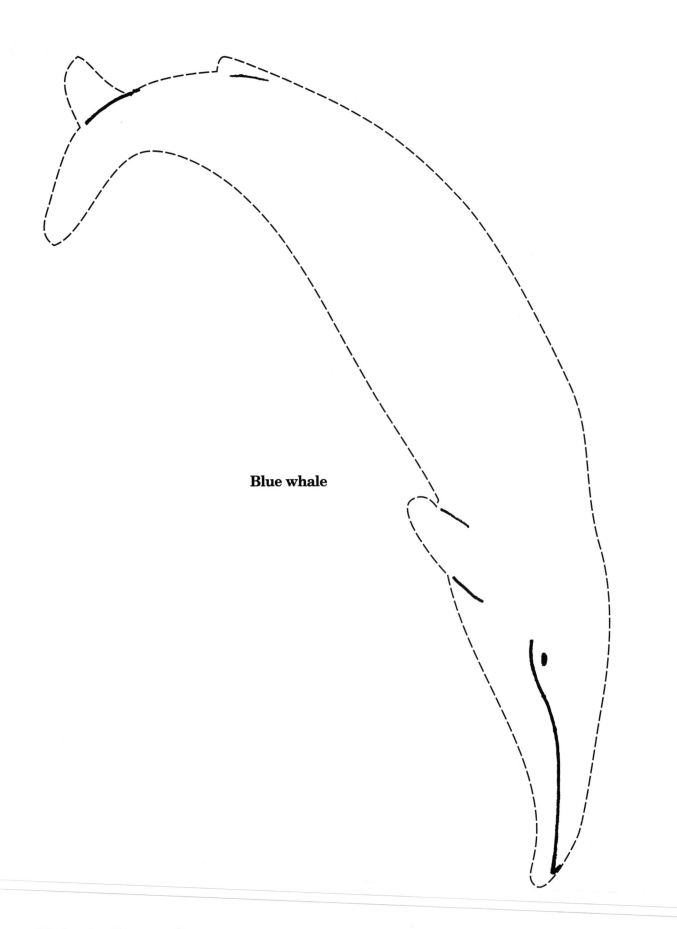

Blue whale

Undersea Creature Pattern

Recommended Books

***Big Al* by Andrew Clements, illustrated by Yoshi** (New York: Picture Book Studio, 1988); full-color illustrations; Interest Level: K-3; Reading Level: 2.0.

Big Al, a blowfish, could not make friends with other fish because of his size and ugliness. When the other fish, however, are captured in a net, Big Al shows his courage and kindness and wins their friendship.

***Evil Under the Sea: A Miss Mallard Mystery* by Robert Quackenbush** (New York: Pippen Press, 1992); full-color illustrations; Interest Level: 3-6; Reading Level: 4.9.

The unsinkable Miss Mallard dons her scuba gear as she seeks to discover the cause of the destruction of the Great Barrier Reef in Australia.

***In Dolphin Time* by Diane Farris** (New York: Four Winds Press, 1994); blue-toned photographs; Interest Level: not listed; Reading Level: 4.7.

In an ethereal, free-form narrative, a child carries home two dolphins who enchant the child's life and who eventually return to the ocean.

***The Magic School Bus on the Ocean Floor* by Joanna Cole, illustrated by Bruce Degan** (New York: Scholastic, 1992); full-color illustrations; Interest Level: K-3; Reading Level: 3.9.

Mrs. Frizzle takes her students on a Magic School Bus field trip to the bottom of the sea, filling the trip with fun and fascinating ocean facts.

***Our Home Is the Sea* by Riki Levinson, illustrated by Dennis Luzak** (New York: E.P. Dutton, 1988); full-color illustrations; Interest Level: K-3; Reading Level: 3.1.

A young Asian boy races home from school in anticipation of seeing his father, a fisherman, return home from a fishing expedition.

***The Rainbow Fish* by Marcus Pfister, translated by J. Alison James** (New York: North-South Books, 1992); full-color and holographic illustrations; Interest Level: K-3; Reading Level: 4.6.

A beautiful yet lonely fish learns that true beauty and friendship consist of sharing and giving.

***The Sea and I* by Harutka Nakawatari, translated by Susan Matsui** (New York: Farrar, Straus & Giroux, 1990); full-color illustrations; Interest Level: K-3; Reading Level: 3.3.

A young boy waits at the seashore for his father to return home from a day of fishing.

***Swimmy* by Leo Lionni** (New York: Pantheon, 1968/1968/1973/1988); full-color illustrations; Interest Level: K-3; Reading Level: 3.0.

A tiny black fish helps a school of tiny red fish overcome their fear of predators and explore the wonders of the sea.

***There's a Sea in My Bedroom* by Margaret Wild, illustrations by Jane Tanner** (New York: Willowisp Press, 1987); Interest Level: K-3; Reading Level: not listed.

A young boy is frightened of the ocean until he imagines that his bedroom has transformed into the sea.

***Whale Song* by Tony Johnston, illustrated by Ed Young** (New York: G.P. Putnam's Sons, 1987); full-color illustrations; Interest Level: K-3; Reading Level: 4.9.

Whales count from one to ten as they sing their songs to each other.

Nonfiction Resources

***Creatures That Glow: This Book Glows in the Dark* by Joann Barkan** (New York: Doubleday, 1991); full-color photographs; Interest Level: 5-8; Reading level: 5.8.

Contains large, bright photographs of animals, primarily sea animals, that glow in the dark. Each photograph is outlined in a chemical that enables it to glow in the dark.

***Going on a Whale Watch* written and illustrated by Bruce McMillan** (New York: Delacorte, 1992); full-color illustrations; Interest Level: K-3; Reading Level: 1.5.

Two young children go on a whale-watching expedition and observe several types of whales.

***Sea Squares* by Joy N. Hulme, illustrated by Carol Schwartz** (New York: Hyperion Books for Children, 1991); full-color illustrations; Interest Level: K-3; Reading Level: 4.8.

Readers are encouraged to practice counting and squaring by using the illustrations of various sea creatures.

***Strange Animals of the Sea (A Pop-up Book)* by Jerry Pinkney** (Washington, DC: National Geographic Society, 1987); full-color illustrations; Interest Level: K-3; Reading Level: 1.5.

Five pages of pop-up pictures and text show the diversity of sea creatures.

***Who's in the Sea? A Sliding Surprise Book* by Charles Reasoner** (Los Angeles: Price Stern Sloan, 1995); full-color illustrations; Interest Level: K-3; Reading Level: not listed.

The author asks questions about a particular sea creature and the reader identifies it by sliding the page to reveal a picture of it.

***Wonders of the Sea* by Louis Sabin, illustrated by Bert Dodson** (Mahwah, NJ: Troll Associates, 1982); full-color illustrations; Interest Level: K-3; Reading Level: 3.3.

The advanced text and watercolor illustrations introduce readers to the varieties of life in the ocean.

Recipe: Fish Patties

1 6-ounce can tuna, drained and flaked

1 10-3/4-ounce can cream of celery soup

1-1/2 cups seasoned bread crumbs

This recipe makes about 14 patties. Mix the above ingredients and shape into 3-inch patties. Fry. Serve hot. CAUTION: This recipe must be prepared by an adult; children may stir the ingredients together and form the patties.

Music Activity: "Undersea Animals"

Use the accompanying movements when singing this song.

UNDERSEA ANIMALS (Sung to the tune "The Friendly Beasts.")

Verse 2: I am the graceful anemone.
I look like a flower and sting like a bee.
I live with my clones in a colony.
I am the graceful anemone.

Verse 3: I am the giant, baleen blue whale.
I steer with my flippers and swim with my tail.
I use my blowhole to in- and exhale.
I am the giant, baleen blue whale.

Verse 4: I am the squid with the ten long arms.
I can change colors to save me from harm.
I can squirt a dark ink when I feel alarm.
I am the squid with the ten long arms.

Verse 5: And all the creatures who live under the sea,
The shark, whale and squid, the anemone,
Must live in nature's harmony,
Must live in nature's harmony.

Finger Play Verses with Movements

Verse 1:   I am the shark with the skin of gray.   *(For both stanzas, move hands, palms*
I glide through the water hunting my prey.   *together, left and right in front of body.)*
I can smell my food from miles away.   *(Point to nose.)*
I am the shark with the skin of gray.   *(Move hands, palms together, left and*
right in front of body.)

Verse 2:   I am the graceful anemone.   *(For both stanzas, cup hands and hold*
I look like a flower and sting like a bee.   *together while wiggling fingers.)*
I live with my clones in a colony.   *(Hold hands close to shoulders while*
wiggling fingers.)

I am the graceful anemone.   *(Cup hands and hold together while*
wiggling fingers.)

Verse 3:   I am the giant, baleen blue whale.   *(For both stanzas, use forefinger to*
I steer with my flippers and   *outline the shape of a whale.)*
swim with my tail.

I use my blowhole to in- and exhale.   *(Point to top of head.)*
I am the giant, baleen blue whale.   *(Use forefinger to outline the shape*
of a whale.)

Verse 4:   I am the squid with the ten long arms.   *(Hold arms down, together and in front*
I can change colors to save me from harm.   *of body, while wiggling fingers.)*
I can squirt a dark ink when I feel alarm.   *(Hold hands, palms out, near shoulders*
as if alarmed.)

I am the squid with the ten long arms.   *(Hold arms down, together and in front*
of body, while wiggling fingers.)

Verse 5:   And all the creatures who live under   *(Bring hands from head to waist while*
the sea.   *wiggling fingers.)*
The shark,   *(Move hands, palms together, left and*
right in front of body.)

Whale   *(Use forefinger to outline the shape*
of a whale.)

And squid,   *(Hold arms down, together and in front*
of the body, while wiggling fingers.)

the anemone.   *(Cup hands together in front of body*
while wiggling fingers.)

Must live in nature's harmony,   *(For both stanzas, hold arms straight*
Must live in nature's harmony.   *above head and slowly move arms*
down and to the side, creating a
large arc.)

Art Activity: Magic Underwater Scene

Materials:

- photocopies of the fish patterns (one fish per child)
- magnetic strip(s)
- 9-inch paper plates (one plate per child)
- glue
- crayons
- safety scissors
- *optional:* variety of dry pasta shapes

Preparation:

Photocopy the fish patterns and cut along the straight lines so that each child receives one fish. Cut the magnetic strip(s) into small squares; a strip measuring 30 inches by 5/8 inch will yield 48 squares measuring 5/8 inch by 5/8 inch. Each child receives two magnetic squares.

Procedure:

Have children color a fish, cut it out, and glue a magnetic square to the back of the fish. Have children color the paper plate to resemble an underwater scene. (*Optional:* Glue dry pasta shapes on the plate to resemble kelp and shells.) When the glue binding the magnetic square to the fish is dry, put the fish on the underwater scene and place the second magnetic square opposite the fish square on the other side of the paper plate. When the second square is moved around the plate, the fish on the other side will appear to be moving on its own volition.

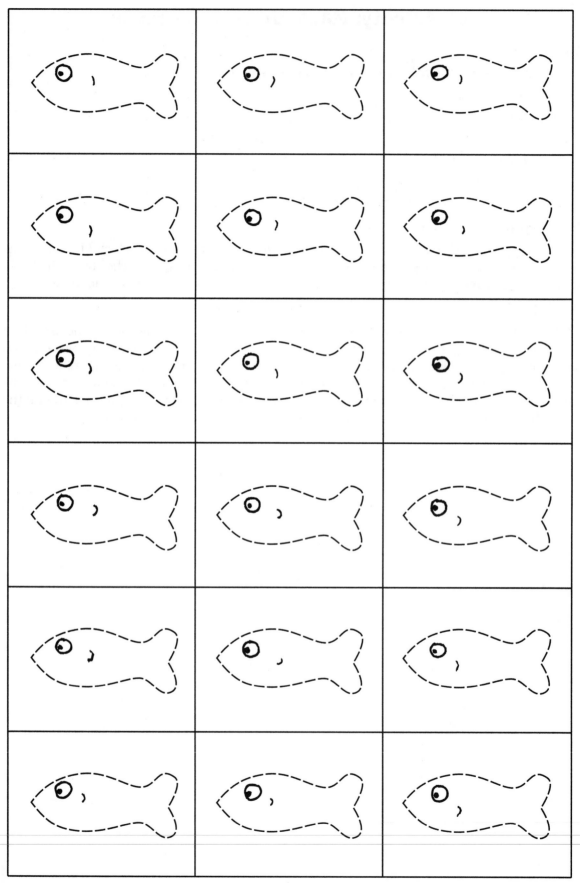

Fish Patterns

Name _____ Date _____

Classroom Teacher _____

Undersea World Research Project: Oceans, rivers, lakes, streams, and ponds provide us with many delicious and nutritious foods. Look in the index of a cookbook under "seafood." How many recipes are listed under "seafood"?

_____

Write the names of three of the most interesting seafood recipes below.

1. _____

2. _____

3. _____

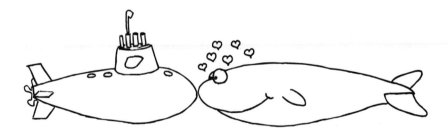

The largest mammal on earth is the blue whale.
It can measure up to 100 feet long.

Vacation

Getting Ready to Teach the Letter V

A week before this unit begins, tell the students that we are going to take a pretend airplane ride and ask them to bring a small suitcase (or backpack) for the trip. Also make an audio tape of an airplane taking off and landing by tape recording a blender or electric mixer set at different speeds.

On the day you plan to teach the unit, arrange the chairs in several rows with an aisle down the center to resemble an airplane cabin. Also, designate an area near the entrance of the library/classroom as the baggage area. Select two students to serve as flight attendants. When students come into the classroom/library, ask the flight attendants to welcome them aboard and help students place their suitcases (or backpacks) in the baggage area.

When everyone is seated, introduce yourself as the pilot, review flight rules, turn on the audio tape, ask the flight attendants to help distribute juice and crackers, and show an in-flight movie in lieu of reading a book. (A good choice is *Angela's Airplane*, available from Filmic Archives, the Cinema Center, Botsford, Connecticut 06404-0386; 1-800-366-1920.) At the conclusion of the movie, explain the rules for disembarking and picking up luggage. The flight attendants help the students line up, retrieve their luggage, and then walk to another section of the library so that you can complete the remaining vacation activities.

Objectives for Vacation:

Each child will be able to:

1. Match the letter "V" with the word "vacation" and vice versa.

2. Summarize the read-aloud story in chronological order.

3. List several means of transportation.

Introductory Activity: Vacation Cutting Story

Photocopy the accompanying pattern on the next page. Fold the photocopied page along the dotted line, holding the blank side toward the audience. As you tell the story, cut along the lines as directed. When finished with the story, open the cut paper to resemble an airplane.

Vacation Story

    (Name of student) is going on vacation, but before he/she goes, he/she has many important errands to run. First, he/she has to pack his/her luggage. He/she especially has to remember to pack his/her hair dryer. I'll cut out a picture of it to help him/her remember. **(Cut from 1 to 2.)**

    (Name of student) also has to go to the library to check out a book. After all, no vacation is complete without a great book. I'll cut out the path he/she took to the library. **(Cut from 2 to 3.)**

    Next, *(name of student)* has to go to the post office and ask the letter carrier to hold his/her mail until he/she returns from vacation. Here's the path he/she took from the library to the post office. **(Cut from 3 to 4.)**

    Finally, *(name of student)* has to go to the travel agency to pick up his/her boarding tickets. How do you think *(name of student)* is going to travel to his/her vacation destination? **(Cut from 4 to 5 and unfold paper to reveal the airplane.)**

1

3

2

4

5

Recommended Books

Are We Almost There? **by James Stevenson** (New York: Greenwillow Books, 1985); full-color illustrations; Interest Level: K-3; Reading Level: 1.0.

Two puppy brothers constantly bicker in the car as their family drives to the beach.

Arthur's Family Vacation **by Marc Brown** (Boston: Little, Brown & Co., 1993); full-color illustrations; Interest Level: K-3; Reading Level: 3.3.

Rain threatens to ruin Arthur's family vacation until the family plans alternate activities.

Emma's Vacation **by David McPhail** (New York: E.P. Dutton, 1987); full-color illustrations; Interest Level: K-3; Reading Level: 1.5.

Despite some setbacks, Emma, a young bear, and her family enjoy an eventful vacation.

First Flight **by David McPhail** (Boston: Little, Brown & Co., 1987); full-color illustrations; Interest Level: K-3; Reading Level: 2.0.

A young boy and his comical bear take their first flight by themselves to Grandma's house.

Flying **by Donald Crews** (New York: Greenwillow Books, 1986); full-color illustrations; Interest Level: K-3; Reading Level: 1.3.

Using simple text, the author follows an airplane on flight from take-off to landing.

Grandma's House **by Elaine Moore, illustrated by Elise Primavera** (New York: Lothrop, Lee & Shepard Books, 1985); full-color illustrations; Interest Level: K-3; Reading Level: 2.9.

A young girl spends a wonderful summer with her grandmother.

Harry's Visit **by Barbara Ann Porte, illustrated by Yossi Abolafia** (New York: Greenwillow Books, 1983); two-color wash over blue; Interest Level: K-3; Reading Level: 2.5.

Despite his reluctance to visit his Aunt Betty, a young boy named Harry enjoys his stay.

Our Puppy's Vacation **by Ruth Brown** (New York: E.P. Dutton, 1987); full-color illustrations; Interest Level: K-3; Reading Level: 2.0.

A puppy exhausts himself romping, exploring, and playing on his first vacation.

The Relatives Came **by Cynthia Rylant, illustrated by Stephen Gammell** (New York: Bradbury Press, 1985/1993); full-color illustrations; Interest Level: K-3; Reading Level: 3.1.

When the relatives from Virginia visit, the extended family bursts with love, laughter, and activity.

Stringbean's Trip to the Shining Sea **by Vera B. Williams and Jennifer Williams** (New York: Greenwillow Books, 1988); full-color illustrations; Interest Level: K-3; Reading Level: 4.3.

Contains a collection of postcards, with letters on the back, from two boys who describe their trip to the west coast.

Nonfiction Resources

Behind the Wheel **by Edward Koren** (New York: Holt, Rinehart & Winston, 1992); black-and-white and full-color illustrations; Interest and Reading Levels: not listed.

Introduces twelve vehicles in operation and includes illustrations of labeled instrumentation. Vehicles include trucks, motorcycles, airplanes, helicopters, buses, and cars.

***New Roads!* by Gail Gibbons** (New York: Thomas Y. Crowell, 1983); full-color illustrations; Interest Level: K-3; Reading Level: 3.5.

Text and detailed illustrations demonstrate how a highway is planned and built. Gibbons wrote several other books that would also be appropriate for this unit, including: *Boat Book, Fill It Up: All About Service Stations,* and *Trains, Trucks and Tunnels.*

***Signs* by Ron and Nancy Goor** (New York: Thomas Y. Crowell, 1983); black-and-white photographs; Interest Level: K-3; Reading Level: 2.1.

Photos and simple text introduce a wide variety of road and building signs and the context in which a person would see them and use them.

***Things That Go: A Traveling Alphabet* by Seymour Reit, illustrated by Fulvio Testa** (New York: Bantam Little Rooster Book, 1990); full-color illustrations; Interest Level: K-3; Reading Level: 2.1.

Illustrations and text introduce the vehicles and other things that go from A to Z.

***Thruway* by Anne and Harlow Rockwell** (New York: Macmillan Publishing Co., 1972); full-color illustrations; Interest Level: K-3; Reading Level: 2.8.

A young boy describes the sights and sounds of driving on a thruway.

Recipe: Vacation Snack Packs

1 cup oatmeal	2-1/2 tablespoons vegetable oil
1/3 cup wheat germ	1 teaspoon vanilla
1/2 cup shredded coconut	1 cup raisins
1/4 cup powdered milk	1 cup peanuts or cashews
1 teaspoon cinnamon	1 cup dried mixed fruit cut into bite-size pieces
2 tablespoons honey	

This recipe makes about 4 cups or 8 1/2-cup servings. Preheat oven to 375 degrees. In a large bowl, mix the first five ingredients. Add honey, oil, and vanilla. Spread on a greased cookie sheet and bake for 8 minutes, stirring the mixture halfway through the baking process. After the mixture has cooled, add raisins, nuts, and dried fruit. Place in small plastic bags.

Music Activity: "Going on Vacation"

Use the accompanying vehicle patterns as templates to trace the eight vehicle shapes onto black felt or construction paper. Tape the felt or paper construction shapes to a globe or world map. Sing the song below, using the accompanying finger plays, and point out the location of the countries and cities mentioned in the song. When the song is finished, you will have been able to circumnavigate the globe.

GOING ON VACATION (Sung to the tune "The Farmer in the Dell.")

Vehicle Patterns

Vehicle Patterns

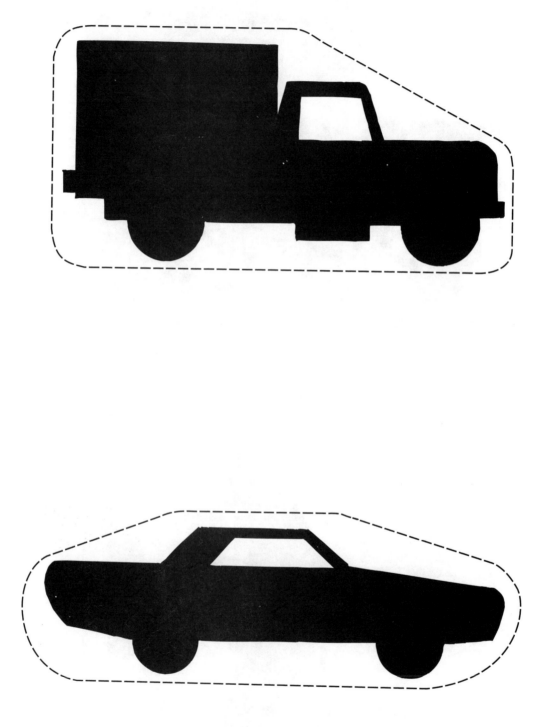

Vehicle Patterns

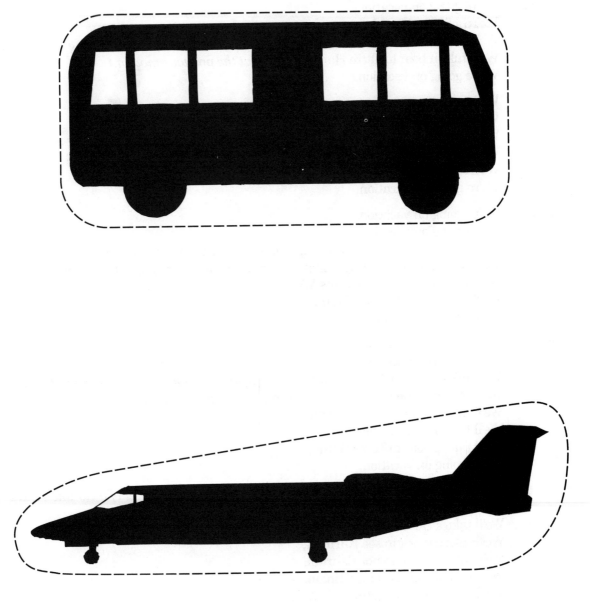

Vehicle Patterns

Finger Play Verses with Movements

Verse 1:   We're going on vacation,
We're going on vacation,
We'll take a boat to Terre Haute,   *(Use hands to imitate waves on water.)*
We're going on vacation.

Verse 2:   We're going on vacation,
We're going on vacation,
We'll take a bike to Germany's Wyk,   *(Use hands to imitate the pedaling motion and*
We'll take a boat to Terre Haute,   *repeat the previous motion.)*
We're going on vacation.

Verse 3:   We're going on vacation,
We're going on vacation,
We'll take a train to sunny Spain,   *(Use hands to imitate the churning wheels of a*
We'll take a bike to Germany's Wyk,   *train and repeat previous motions.)*
We'll take a boat to Terre Haute,
We're going on vacation.

Verse 4:   We're going on vacation,
We're going on vacation,
We'll take a plane to hot Bahrain,   *(Hold out arms to imitate the wings of an*
We'll take a train to sunny Spain,   *airplane and repeat previous motions.)*
We'll take a bike to Germany's Wyk,
We'll take a boat to Terre Haute,
We're going on vacation.

Verse 5:   We're going on vacation,
We're going on vacation,
We'll take a truck to see Kurmuk,   *(Pretend to be riding on a bumpy road and*
We'll take a plane to hot Bahrain,   *repeat previous motions.)*
We'll take a train to sunny Spain,
We'll take a bike to Germany's Wyk,
We'll take a boat to Terre Haute,
We're going on vacation.

Verse 6:   We're going on vacation,   *(Pretend to steer the wheel of a car and repeat*
We're going on vacation,   *previous motion.)*
We'll take a car to Zanzibar,
We'll take a truck to see Kurmuk,
We'll take a plane to hot Bahrain,
We'll take a train to sunny Spain,
We'll take a bike to Germany's Wyk,
We'll take a boat to Terre Haute,
We're going on vacation.

Verse 7: We're going on vacation,
We're going on vacation,
We'll take a bus to dry Zanthus,
We'll take a car to Zanzibar,
We'll take a truck to see Kurmuk,
We'll take a plane to hot Bahrain,
We'll take a train to sunny Spain,
We'll take a bike to Germany's Wyk,
We'll take a boat to Terre Haute,
We're going on vacation.

(Pretend to wave from a bus window and repeat previous motions.)

Verse 8: We're going on vacation,
We're going on vacation,
We'll take a jet to Joliet,
We'll take a bus to dry Zanthus,
We'll take a car to Zanzibar,
We'll take a truck to see Kurmuk,
We'll take a plane to hot Bahrain,
We'll take a train to sunny Spain,
We'll take a bike to Germany's Wyk,
We'll take a boat to Terre Haute,
And then return to home.

(Raise hand through the air to imitate a jet taking off and repeat previous motions.)

(Use fingers to outline the shape of a house or building.)

Art Activity: Cameras

Materials:

- photocopies of the camera pattern (one photocopy per child)
- yarn cut into 18-inch lengths (one length per child)
- white 8-1/2 x 11-inch paper
- paper punch
- crayons or fine-tipped colored felt markers
- X-acto™ knife

Preparation:

Photocopy the camera pattern. Cut additional paper into strips measuring 11-inch by 2-1/8-inch (two strips per child) to be used as film. Fold cameras at the fold line. Use a paper punch to cut out holes for the neck strap. Insert yarn ends in the holes and tie to create a neck strap for the camera. Use an X-acto™ knife to cut along the two dotted lines at the back of the camera.

Procedure:

Distribute the camera. Have students insert the paper strips in the back of the camera. Children can pretend to snap a picture, then draw the picture on their "film." When the "film" is removed from the camera, it should contain a series of hand-drawn pictures.

Camera Pattern

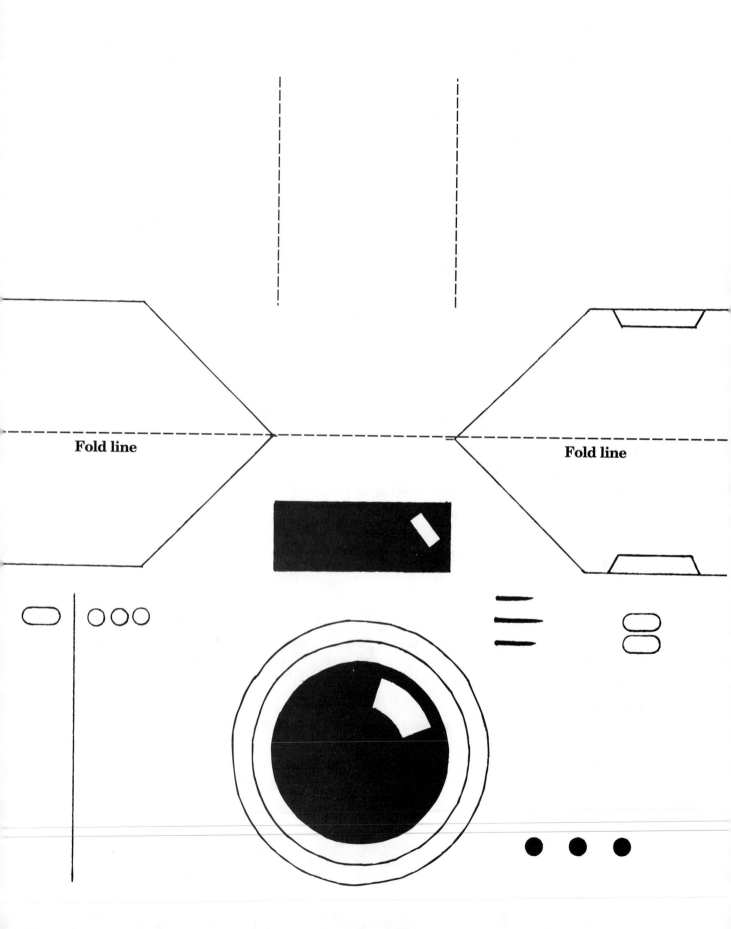

Fold line

Fold line

Name _____ Date _____

Classroom Teacher _____

Vacation Research Project: Many people who travel on vacation employ the services of a travel agency. Use the Yellow Pages of your telephone directory to look up "travel agency." List up to five travel agencies and their telephone numbers below.

1. Name of agency _____

   Telephone number _____

2. Name of agency _____

   Telephone number _____

3. Name of agency _____

   Telephone number _____

4. Name of agency _____

   Telephone number _____

5. Name of agency _____

   Telephone number _____

Write the name of the telephone directory where you found your information.

_____

What is gray and has big ears, a
tail and a trunk?

A mouse on a vacation!

Weather

Getting Ready to Teach the Letter W

Bring various outer wear to the library to help introduce the unit. When students enter the library, wear a raincoat and carry an umbrella. Also dim the lights and play an audio tape of a rainstorm. ("Torrential Thunderstorm" is available from Outlet Book Company, 225 Park Avenue South, New York, New York 10003; "Wilderness Thunderstorm" is available from NorthWord Press, Inc., P.O. Box 1360, Minocqua, Wisconsin 54548, 1-800-336-5666.) Discuss how we dress to meet different weather conditions. Next, dress one of the students in a heavy coat, boots, and gloves, and ask students to guess which weather condition calls for this type of clothes. Repeat the procedure, this time using shorts, sunglasses, and a sun hat.

Objectives for Weather:

Each child will be able to:

1. Match the letter "W" with the word "weather" and vice versa.

2. Summarize the read-aloud story in chronological order.

3. Name and describe several weather conditions.

Introductory Activity: Weather Forecast

Materials:

- one large piece of felt
- scissors
- crayons
- glue
- one photocopy each of map and disk patterns

Preparation:

Enlarge and trace the United States map onto a large piece of felt and cut out. Affix the felt map to the chalkboard. Cut out six 3-inch felt disks. Color and cut out the six weather symbols. Glue the symbols to the felt disks.

Procedure:

Present a mock television forecast to the students, placing the weather symbol disks on the felt map as you discuss various weather conditions. Choose individual students to present their own weather forecasts using the disks and map. This activity is an excellent opportunity to videotape the students, but don't force any student to be taped if he or she is not comfortable with the idea.

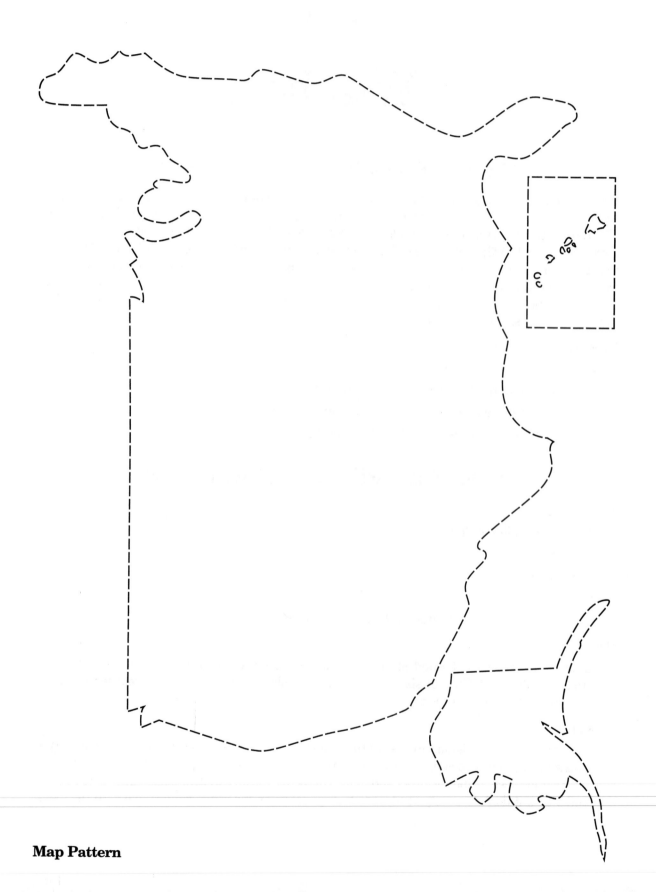

Map Pattern

Rain

Snow

Cloudy

Sunny

Windy

Thunderstorm

Disk Patterns

Recommended Books

Clifford and the Big Storm **by Norman Bridwell** (New York: Scholastic, 1995); full-color illustrations; Interest Level: K-3; Reading Level: not listed.

Clifford, an enormous red dog, saves Grandmother's house when a tornado threatens to destroy it.

Cloudy with a Chance of Meatballs **by Judi Barrett, illustrated by Ron Barrett** (New York: Aladdin Books, 1978); full-color illustrations; Interest Level: K-3; Reading Level: 3.2.

A grandfather tells his children about the land of Chewandswallow where it rains orange juice and snows mashed potatoes. Eventually, however, the weather spins out of control, threatening the town and its residents.

Geraldine's Big Snow **by Holly Keller** (New York: Scholastic, 1988); full-color illustrations; Interest Level: K-3; Reading Level: 2.3.

A young pig named Geraldine waits in breathless anticipation for the season's first snow.

Henry and Mudge in the Sparkle Day **by Cynthia Rylant, illustrated by Susie Stevenson** (New York: Simon and Schuster, 1988); full-color illustrations; Interest Level: K-3; Reading Level: 3.0.

A boy and his dog enjoy the magic of snow, the excitement of Christmas, and a nighttime walk.

Peter and the North Wind **retold by Freya Littledale, illustrated by Troy Howell** (New York: Scholastic, 1971 text/1988 illustrations); full-color illustrations; Interest Level: K-3; Reading Level: 2.5.

The North Wind gives a young boy a magic cloth, a goat, and a stick—which are stolen by a greedy innkeeper. The boy, however, outwits the innkeeper and retrieves the stolen items.

The Sea-Breeze Hotel **by Marcia Vaughan and Patricia Mullins** (New York: HarperCollins, 1992); full-color illustrations; Interest Level: K-3; Reading Level: 5.5.

The Sea-Breeze Hotel has no guests because of the blustery wind until a young boy named Sam builds and flies kites that attract many guests.

The Sky Is Full of Song, **poems selected by Lee Bennett Hopkins, illustrated by Dirk Zimmer** (New York: Harper & Row, 1983); Interest Level: 3-6; Reading Level: 4.2.

Contains an anthology of 38 short poems describing the seasons.

Something Is Going to Happen **by Charlotte Zolotow, illustrated by Catherine Stock** (New York: Harper & Row, 1988); full-color illustrations; Interest Level: K-3; Reading Level: 4.5.

A family wakes on a November morning to the magic of the season's first snow.

That Sky, That Rain **by Carolyn Otto, illustrations by Megan Lloyd** (New York: Harper Trophy, 1990); full-color illustrations; Interest Level: K-3; Reading Level: 1.8.

A young girl and her grandmother prepare the farm animals for a rain shower.

The Wind Blew **by Pat Hutchins** (New York: Scholastic, 1993); full-color illustrations; Interest Level: K-3; Reading Level: 3.3.

In this cumulative rhyming tale, various people follow the wind as it picks up their umbrellas, letters, newspapers, and other possessions.

Nonfiction Resources

***Clouds* by Roy Wandelmaier, illustrated by John Jones** (Mahwah, NJ: Troll Associates, 1985); full-color illustrations; Interest Level: K-3; Reading Level: 1.9.

Contains names and descriptions of different types of clouds and the weather they bring.

***Rain* by Robert Kalan, illustrated by Donald** Crews (New York: Scholastic, 1978); full-color illustrations; Interest Level: K-3; Reading Level: 1.2.

Simple text and clever illustrations chart a rainstorm as it travels through the countryside.

***Weather* by Gallimard Jeunesse and Pascale de Bourgoing, illustrated by Sophie Kniffke** (New York: Scholastic, 1989); full-color illustrations; Interest Level: K-3; Reading Level: 2.2.

Transparent pages and simple explanations are used to illustrate various weather conditions.

***What Will the Weather Be?* by Lynda DeWitt, illustrated by Carolyn Croll** (New York: HarperCollins, 1991); illustrated; Interest Level: K-3; Reading Level: 3.5.

Explains how weather conditions develop and how meteorologists forecast weather.

***What Will the Weather Be Like Today?* by Paul Rogers, illustrated by Kazuko** (New York: Greenwillow Books, 1989); full-color illustrations; Interest Level: K-3; Reading Level: 1.6.

Various animals, in rhyming verse, describe the variations of weather.

Recipe: Rainbow in a Cloud

> 1 3-ounce box blueberry gelatin
>
> 1 cup boiling water
>
> 1 cup cool water
>
> 1 8-ounce container non-dairy whipped topping
>
> 1 small container nonpareils or rainbow-colored candy sprinkles

This recipe serves 4. Mix gelatin according to directions. Pour 1/2 cup mixture into four 7-ounce clear plastic cups. Place in the refrigerator and allow to jell. Put a dollop of whipped topping in each glass and sprinkle with nonpareils.

Music Activity: "Weather Is . . ."

Use the accompanying movements when you sing this song.

WEATHER IS . . . (Sung to the tune "The Old Gray Mare.")

Finger Play Verses with Movements

Weather is a soft and gentle springtime rain,	*(Move hands in front of body from head to waist while wiggling fingers.)*
A twisty, turny hurricane,	*(Twist torso left and right.)*
Jack Frost at the windowpane.	*(Cup hands around eyes as if peering through a window.)*
Weather is the wind that blows the weather vane.	*(Place hands, palms together, in front of body and point hands left and right.)*
Weather is all of these.	*(Hold arms straight above head and slowly move the arms down and to the side, creating a large arch.)*
Ice storms and snow and sleet,	*(Hug yourself while pretending to shiver and shake.)*
Hot, humid summer heat.	*(Use one hand to fan face.)*
Weather is a soft and gentle summer rain.	*(Move arms in front of body from head to waist while wiggling fingers.)*
Weather is all of these.	*(Hold arms straight above head and slowly move arms down and to the side, creating a large arch.)*

Art Activity: Rainbow Bookmark

Materials:

- blue posterboard cut into 3-inch by 6-inch rectangles
- red, yellow, green, and blue yarn cut into 6-inch lengths
- cotton balls (one per student)
- glue
- paper punch
- *optional:* silver glitter

Preparation:

Punch four holes at the bottom of the posterboard rectangle.

Procedure:

Have students shred a cotton ball and glue it on their bookmark to represent a cloud. Tie a different color of yarn through each hole to represent a rainbow. *Optional:* Glue silver glitter on the bookmark to represent rain. CAUTION: Closely supervise the children when working with glitter.

Name _____ Date _____

Classroom Teacher _____

Weather Research Project: Look in your newspaper to find the weather section. Write tomorrow's forecast on the lines below.

_____

_____

_____

_____

_____

_____

Write the name of the newspaper where you found your information.

_____

Celebrate Weatherman's Day on February 5.

"X-tra" Ideas

Book Movers

Trace the pictures at the end of this section onto white posterboard and color them. Insert the characters in appropriate books, allowing the nose and hands to protrude onto the cover of the book as shown in the illustration below. Place the books on display.

Bookmark Factory

Sometimes libraries are asked to set up booths for community fairs or school fund-raisers. A simple, people-pleasing idea for such a booth display is a bookmark factory. Stock your "factory" with unlined colored index cards, paper punches, colored yarn cut into 6-inch lengths, stamps and stamp pads, and stickers. (Ellison Educational, P.O. Box 8209, Newport Beach, California 92658, 1-800-253-2238, sells a variety of hand-held paper punches. Kidstamps, P.O. Box 18699, Cleveland Heights, Ohio 44118 sells children's literature-based stamps.) Browsers can use the stamps, paper punches, and stickers to decorate the index cards, punching holes in the bottom of the card to insert yarn fringe.

Collaborative School/Public Library Reading Program

School and public libraries can create a reading partnership program to benefit children. First, choose a motto and a theme such as "Be a Grand Slam Reader." Design a certificate and purchase a large quantity of tiny stickers that reflect the theme. Purchase an inexpensive prize, which can be autographed, for each classroom. Send a letter to a variety of well-known persons, such as the governor, sports figures and television personalities, asking each person to autograph one of the prizes as part of the reading project. If the person agrees to participate, send the person the prize along with return postage and a letter of appreciation. Place one autographed prize in each classroom to serve as an incentive when the project begins.

Create a chart featuring every child's name and then place the chart in a common area in the school. Advertise the program with bulletin boards, displays, and bookmarks. Send a letter to parents and teachers outlining the program. Explain that on a given date, students will be offered an opportunity to check out public library books over a six-week period. Also explain that all participants will receive a reading certificate and students who check out and read the greatest number of books may win an additional prize.

When the program begins, the public librarian will give each participant one sticker for each book he/she checks out. The child is to place those stickers by his/her name on the chart at school. At the end of the six-week period, conduct an awards assembly and distribute participation certificates as well as the autographed prizes for the student in each classroom who checked out and read the greatest number of books.

Creative Dramatics

Use book/cassette tapes of familiar fairy tales as the basis for creative dramatics. (Educational Record Center, Inc., 3233 Burnt Mill Drive, Suite 100, Wilmington, North Carolina 28403-2655, 1-800-438-1637, sells a wide variety of book/cassette kits.) The children first listen to the book/cassette. Then assign parts, briefly explaining basic directions. Then turn on the cassette again and have the children pantomime the story.

Other classics that lend themselves well to creative dramatics are:

The Mitten: A Ukranian Folktale by Jan Brett (New York: Putnam, 1990)

Millions of Cats by Wanda Gag (New York: Putnam, 1977/1996)

Caps for Sale by Esphyr Slobodkina (New York: Scholastic, 1993)

The Sneetches & Other Stories by Dr. Seuss (New York: Random Books for Young Readers, 1966)

Display Sign

Looking for an inexpensive, eye-catching display sign? Decorate pink flamingo lawn ornaments and hang a sign around their necks to advertise upcoming events. Place a styrofoam ball in each of two matching shoes and insert the flamingo's leg spikes into the balls. The flamingos can be decorated in school colors, hats, and T-shirts to boost the local sports team or seasonal costumes to celebrate holidays. A white satin cape, white-rimmed sunglasses, and rhinestones glued on white sneakers can create an Elvis Presley Flamingo to introduce books about music and singers.

Pencil Retrievers

If you find yourself losing quantities of pencils, require that children leave a shoe as collateral for the pencil. When the pencil is returned, return the shoe. Also, have several potted plants placed in old shoes throughout the library as a comical reminder to return all library pencils.

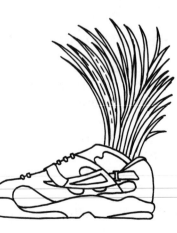

THIS BOOK IS TOPS!

Book Mover

SAIL THIS
BOOK TO
ADVENTURE!

Book Mover

Getting Ready to Teach the Letter Y

This unit presents a wonderful opportunity for children to bring in their baby pictures and guess each other's identity. You also could ask other teachers to contribute their baby photos and the name of their favorite childhood book for an interesting display or bulletin board.

Objectives for You:

Each child will be able to:

1. Match the letter "Y" with the word "you" and vice versa.

2. Summarize the read-aloud story in chronological order.

3. Define himself or herself using a variety of descriptors.

Introductory Activity: Message Rebus

Materials:

- crayons
- scissors
- glue
- magnetic strips
- rebus patterns

Preparation:

Color and cut out the rebus patterns. Glue a magnetic strip to the back of each rebus so that it can be affixed to the chalkboard.

Procedure:

Explain the meaning of each rebus symbol as you place the symbol on the chalkboard. Use the symbols to create a message for one of the children. (Suggested messages are listed below.) Have children, one at a time, create positive "love" messages for each other on the chalkboard with the rebusses.

Rebus Messages

1. You are an angel.
2. You are very (bear-e) lucky.
3. You are a lucky ducky.
4. You are a dear.
5. You are a star.

6. You are lucky.
7. You are a peach.
8. You are keen.
9. You are peachy keen.
10. You are a lucky star.

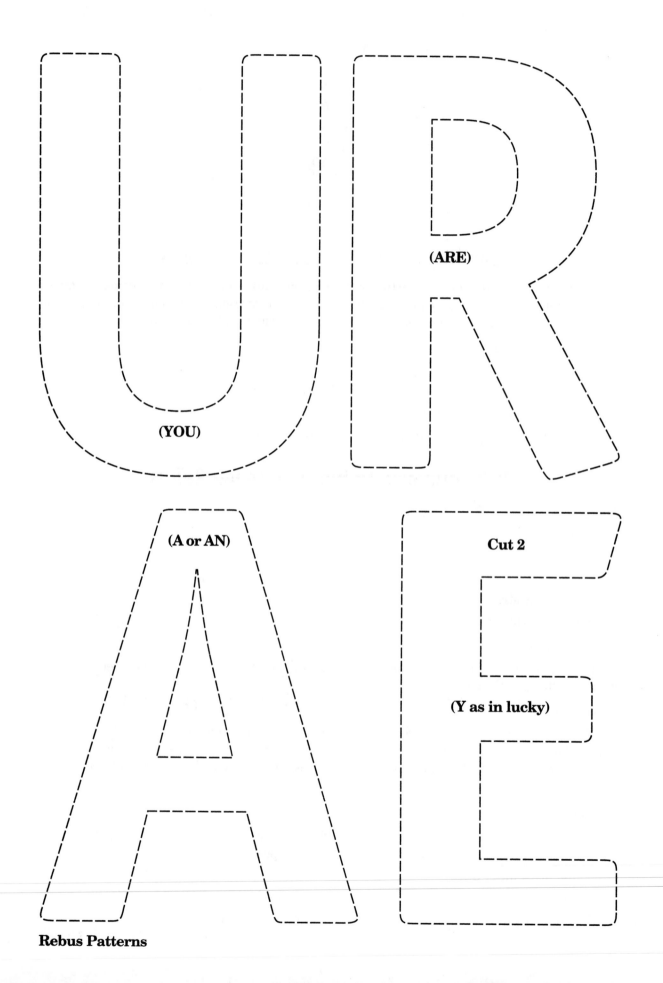

(ARE)

(YOU)

(A or AN)

Cut 2

(Y as in lucky)

Rebus Patterns

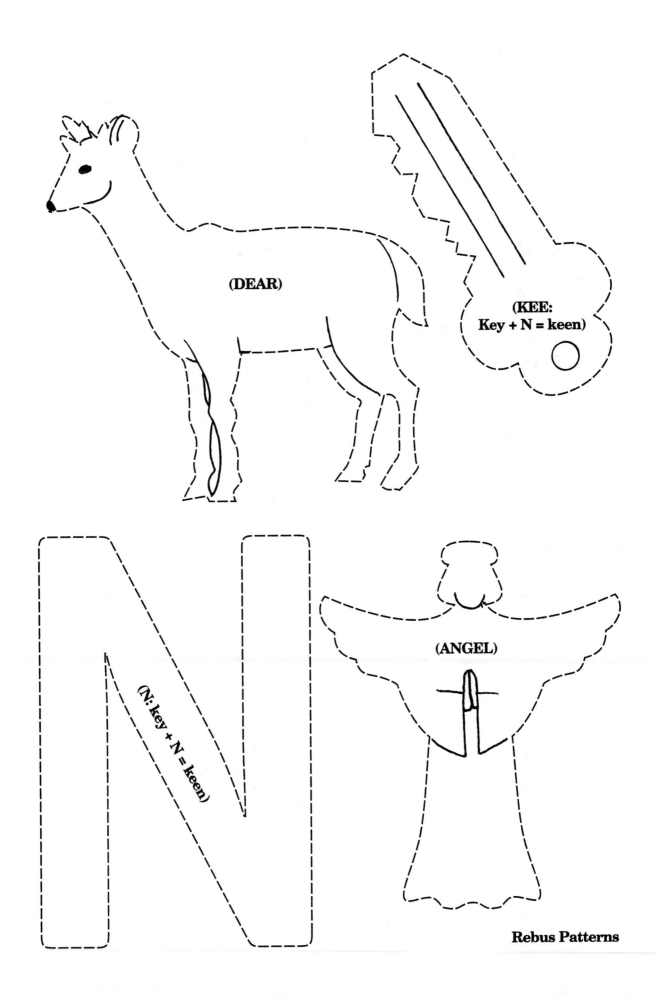

(DEAR)

(KEE:
Key + N = keen)

(N: key + N = keen)

(ANGEL)

Rebus Patterns

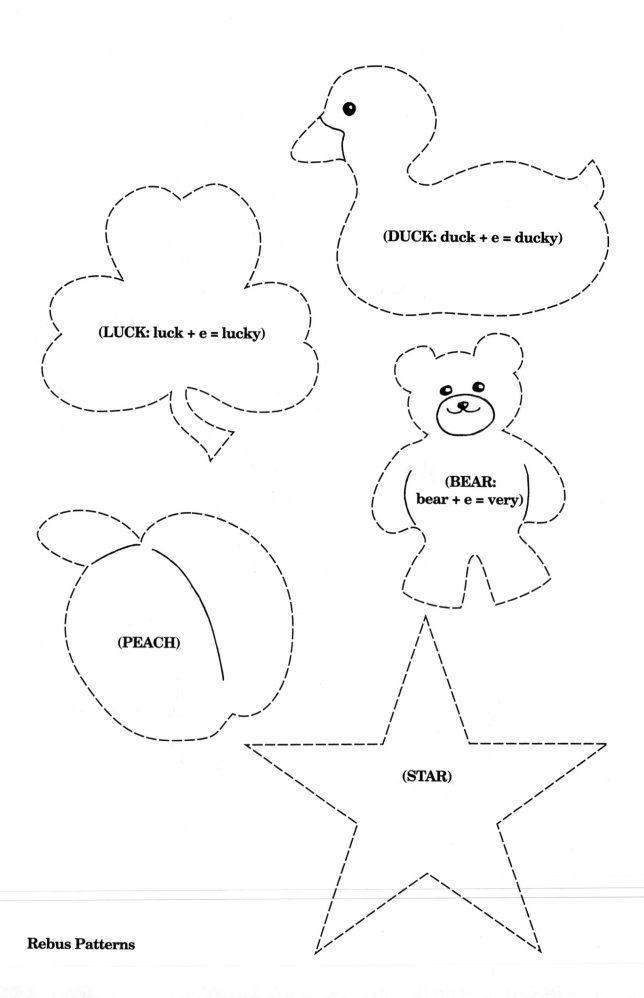

(DUCK: duck + e = ducky)

(LUCK: luck + e = lucky)

(BEAR:
bear + e = very)

(PEACH)

(STAR)

Rebus Patterns

Recommended Books

Albert's Toothache **by Barbara Williams, illustrated by Kay Chorao** (New York: E.P. Dutton & Co., 1974); black-and-white illustrations; Interest Level: K-3; Reading Level: 2.7.

A young turtle named Albert worries his parents when he announces he has a toothache.

All I Am **by Eileen Roe, illustrated by Helen Cogancherry** (New York: Bradbury Press, 1990); full-color illustrations; Interest Level: K-3; Reading Level: 1.3.

A young child describes his many roles and talents.

Here Are My Hands **by Bill Martin, Jr. and John Archembault, illustrated by Ted Rand** (New York: Holt, 1987); full-color illustrations; Interest Level: K-3; Reading Level: 2.0.

Simple, poetic text and bright illustrations teach the reader about the parts of the body including the head, hands, feet, nose, ears, eyes, and neck.

Let's Do It **by Amy MacDonald, illustrated by Maureen Roffey** (Cambridge, MA: Candlewick Press, 1992); full-color illustrations; Interest and Reading Levels: not listed.

The reader is encouraged to identify body parts by touching his or her nose, finding his or her eyes, waving bye-bye, etc.

My Doctor **by Harlow Rockwell** (New York: Macmillan Publishing Co., 1973); full-color illustrations; Interest Level: K-3; Reading Level: 2.9.

Using simple text and illustrations, a young boy describes his doctor's tools and how they are used.

My Hands Can **by Jean Holzenthaler, illustrated by Nancy Tafuri** (New York: E.P. Dutton, 1978); full-color illustrations; Interest Level: K-3; Reading Level: 1.9.

This book shows all the things hands can do.

My Tooth Is Loose! **by Martin Silverman, illustrated by Amy Aitken** (New York: Viking, 1991/1994); full-color illustrations; Interest Level: K-3; Reading Level: 1.6.

A group of friends suggests ways for Georgie to pull out his loose tooth. His mother, however, reassures him that his tooth will fall out by itself—and it does.

Oh, Baby! **by Sara Stein, photographs by Holly Anne Shelowitz** (New York: Walker and Company, 1993); full-color illustrations; Interest Level: K-3; Reading Level: 3.1.

Humorous photographs and simple text chronicle a baby's development from birth to toddlerhood.

On Monday When It Rained **by Cherryl Kachenmeister, photographs by Tom Berthiaune** (Boston: Houghton Mifflin Co., 1989); black-and-white photographs; Interest Level: K-3; Reading Level: 1.6.

Presents everyday situations and a young boy's emotional responses to those situations.

Tommy Goes to the Doctor **by Gunilla Wolde** (Boston: Houghton Mifflin Co., 1972); full-color illustrations; Interest Level: K-3; Reading Level: not listed.

A young boy visits the doctor for a routine exam.

Nonfiction Resources

***A Book About Your Skeleton* by Ruth Belov Gross, illustrated by Steve Bjorkman** (New York: Scholastic, 1978/1979/1994); full-color illustrations; Interest Level: K-3; Reading Level: 3.0.

Humorously introduces readers to the functions, types, composition, and growth patterns of bones.

***A Doctor's Tools* by Kenny DeSantis, photographs by Patricia Agre** (New York: Dodd, Mead & Co., 1985); black-and-white photographs; Interest Level: 3-6; Reading Level: 4.2.

Spotlights 18 doctor's tools and how and why they are used.

***My First Book of the Body* by Chuck Murphy** (New York: Scholastic, 1995); full-color illustrations; Interest Level: Preschool; Reading Level: not listed.

Lift-the-flaps and pop-ups pose and answer questions about the human body.

***Sense Suspense: A Guessing Game for the Five Senses* by Bruce Mcmillan** (New York: Macmillan, 1994); full-color illustrations and photographs; Interest Level: K-3; Reading Level: not listed.

In this almost wordless picture book, photographs depict children using their senses while engaged in various activities. Children identify how each sense would interpret each situation.

***What's Inside? My Body* by Angela Royston, photographs by Steve Gorton and Paul Bricknell, illustrated by Richard Manning** (Boston: Dorling Kindersley, 1991); full-color illustrations; Interest and Reading Levels: not listed.

Contains basic information about the parts of the body.

Recipe: You Are My Sunshine Salad

1 20-ounce can pineapple rings

4 carrots, shredded

1 16-ounce container cottage cheese **or** 1 quart sherbet

1 head lettuce

1 small box raisins

1 8-ounce bottle maraschino cherries, sliced

This recipe serves 10. Place a lettuce leaf on each of ten salad plates. Place a pineapple ring on each leaf. Divide shredded carrots into ten equal portions and arrange each portion around a pineapple ring. Place a small scoop (such as a coffee measure scoop) of cottage cheese or sherbet in the middle of each ring. Use raisins and cherries to create a face on the cottage cheese or sherbet.

Music Activity: "The Guessing Game"

This song is used for a guessing game activity. The singer, without telling anyone else, is to select a child as the object of the song. The singer then sings the song, making up verses that serve as clues for the children. (The verse accompanying this song is an example.) At the end of the song, children are to raise their hand and guess who was the object of the song. Continue as before for other children.

THE GUESSING GAME
(Sung to the tune "She'll Be Coming 'Round the Mountain.")

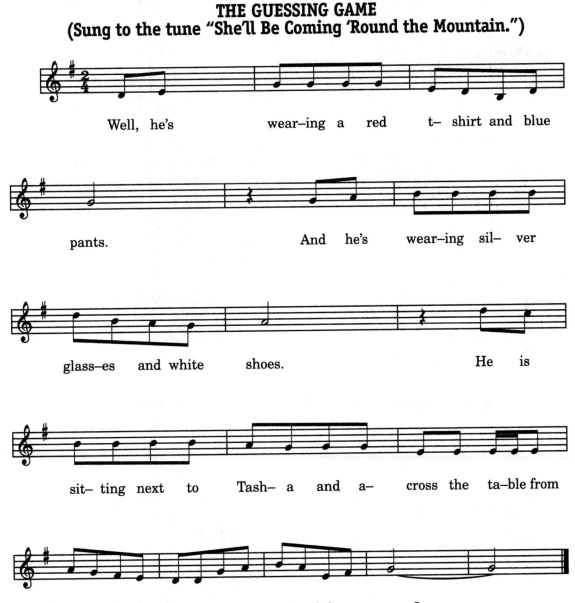

Thom—as, Do you know the secret per—son? Can you guess?

Art Activity: "You Are a Star" Shoe Pals

Materials:
- yellow felt
- scissors
- felt scraps
- glue
- glitter, sequins, feathers, etc.
- star pattern

Preparation:

Using the star pattern below as a template, trace and cut out stars from yellow felt, two stars per child. Cut two slits in the middle of the star as shown on the template.

Procedure:

Have the students decorate felt stars with glitter, sequins, or feathers. (Or they could use felt scraps, sequins, and glitter to decorate paper stars.) Place a star on each child's shoes, securing it to the shoe by pulling the shoestrings through the slits and tying. *CAUTION:* Closely supervise the children if using glitter.

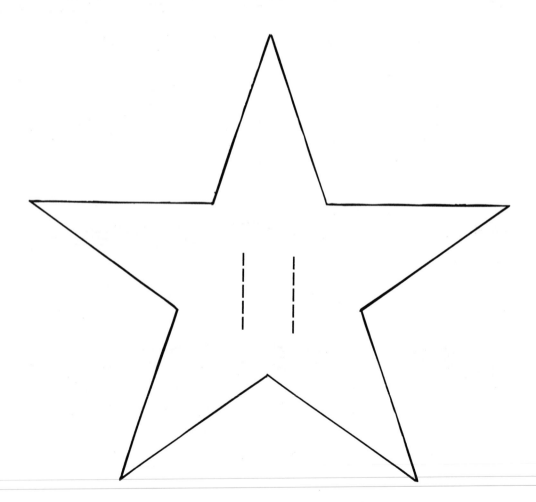

Name _____ Date _____

Classroom Teacher _____

You Research Project: Look up your last name in the white pages of a telephone directory. Answer the questions below.

1. Is your family's name listed in the telephone directory?

   _____

2. How many families in the telephone directory have your last name?

   _____

3. Do you know any of the other families with your last name who are listed in the telephone directory?

   _____

Write the name of the telephone directory where you found your information.

   _____

Birds on a telephone wire

Getting Ready to Teach the Letter Z

This unit lends itself to creating a stuffed animal zoo. Encourage children to bring in their favorite stuffed animal for display. The animals can be grouped by those that share the same environment (oceans, mountains, polar regions, tropical forests, grasslands, deserts, and temperate forests) or those of the same species. If the animals are grouped according to species, it might be interesting to share the group name of some familiar species:

A group of antelope is a *herd*.

A group of bears is a *sloth*.

A group of beavers is a colony or *family*.

A group of cats is a clutter or *clowder*.

A group of cattle is a *drove*.

A group of chickens is a *flock* or *brood*.

A group of deer is a *herd*.

A group of dogs is a *kennel*.

A group of donkeys is a *pace*.

A group of ducks is a *brace*.

A group of elephants is a *herd*.

A group of foxes is a *leash* or *skulk*.

A group of geese is a *flock* or *gaggle*.

A group of giraffes is a *herd*.

A group of goats is a *herd*.

A group of hogs is a *herd* or *drove*.

A group of horses is a *team*.

A group of kangaroos is a *herd, troop,* or *mob*.

A group of lions is a *pride*.

A group of nightingales is a *watch*.

A group of ostriches is a *flock*.

A group of pigs is a *litter*.

A group of rabbits is a *warren*.

A group of seals is a *trip* or *herd*.

A group of sheep is a *block, flock,* or *herd*.

A group of swans is a *flock*.

A group of turkeys is a *flock*.

A group of whales is a *pod*.

A group of wolves is a *pack*.

A group of zebras is a *herd*.

Here are some other interesting animal facts:

- Scientists have identified more than a million kinds of animals, but hundreds of new animals are discovered each year.
- The blue whale, which can grow 100 feet long, is the largest animal.
- The Indian swift can fly up to 200 miles per hour while the sea horse travels 10 inches per minute.
- The sun jellyfish has tentacles over 200 feet long.
- The African elephant has the largest ears of all animals, measuring 4 feet across.
- The Arctic tern travels 25,000 miles as it migrates from the North Pole to South Pole and back.
- The largest snake is the anaconda, which can grow over 25 feet long.

- A cougar is also called a bearcat, panther, puma, or mountain lion.
- The first known zoo was established in China about 1,000 years ago.

Objectives for Zoo:

Each child will be able to:

1. Match the letter "Z" with the word "zoo."
2. Summarize the read-aloud story in chronological order.
3. List a variety of animals that live at the zoo.

Introductory Activity: Zoo Game

Materials:

- photocopies of zoo animals
- scissors
- hole puncher
- 18-inch lengths of yarn
- the "Zoo Story"

Preparation:

Photocopy enough copies of the zoo animals so that each child receives one animal. Separate the animals by cutting along the dotted lines. Punch a hole at the top of each animal picture, thread an 18-inch length of yarn through the picture, and the yarn at the top to make an animal necklace.

Procedure:

Give each child—except one—an animal necklace; the child not receiving a necklace will be the key character in the zoo story. Make sure each child knows the name of his or her animal. Explain that you are going to read a story. (The story is given with this activity.) Every time a child hears the name of his or her animal, that child is to stand up, turn around in a circle, and then sit down again. Every time the children hear the word "zoo" in the story, the entire class is to carefully and quietly switch seats. The key character is to stand up, turn around, and sit down every time he or she hears his or her name in the story.

Zoo Animals

Zoo Story

(**NAME OF CHILD**) was very excited. He/she was going to visit the **ZOO.** He/she wanted to see the **COBRA.** He/she wanted to wave to the **BEAR** and the **LION.** And he/she wanted to say hello to the **GIRAFFE** and **ZEBRA.** But most of all, he/she wanted to visit Elmer the Baby **ELEPHANT.** The last time (**NAME OF CHILD**) had visited, the keeper had let (**NAME OF CHILD**) help him/her give Elmer the Baby **ELEPHANT** a bath.

Finally, the big day arrived. (**NAME OF CHILD**) ran to the gate and gave the gatekeeper his/her ticket into the **ZOO.** He/she ran to the **COBRA's** cage and watched him sleeping. He/she raced to the **BEAR's** cage and waved. Then he/she walked to the **LION's** place and watched him sunning himself. (**NAME OF CHILD**) sauntered to the **ZEBRA's** area and watched him eat his lunch. Then he/she saw the **GIRAFFE** care for her baby.

Finally, (**NAME OF CHILD**) came to Elmer the Baby **ELEPHANT's** place. Elmer was getting another bath. And the baby was much, much larger. (**NAME OF CHILD**) leaned against the fence to get a better look.

"Elmer," (**NAME OF CHILD**) called. "Do you remember me?"

Elmer raised his head and flapped his enormous ears. Then he filled his trunk with water and playfully sprayed the water at (**NAME OF CHILD**). (**NAME OF CHILD**) was soaked from head to foot and very, very embarrassed.

(**NAME OF CHILD**) ran away, past the **GIRAFFE** and **ZEBRA,** around the **BEAR's** cave, **COBRA's** cage and **LION's** den. Just then, the keeper saw him/her.

"(**NAME OF CHILD**)," the keeper asked. "What happened to you?"

"Elmer the **ELEPHANT** saw me," (**NAME OF CHILD**) replied, "and gave me a bath."

"No wonder," the keeper laughed. "He remembers the bath you gave him and he just returned the favor for you. After all, an **ELEPHANT** never forgets."

(**NAME OF CHILD**) chuckled. "I'll remember that the next time I visit the zoo."

Recommended Books

***Bobby's Zoo* by Carolyn Lunn, illustrated by Tom Dunnington** (Chicago: Children's Press, 1989); full-color illustrations; Interest Level: K-3; Reading Level: 1.8.

A young boy, whose house is filled with animals, opens a zoo at his home.

***The Camel Who Left the Zoo* by Pascale Allamand, English version by Michael Bullock** (New York: Charles Scribner's Sons, 1976); full-color illustrations; Interest Level: K-3; Reading Level: 2.9.

Hundreds and hundreds of birds help Camel and the other animals in the zoo escape to freedom in their native countries.

***A Children's Zoo* by Tana Hoban** (New York: Greenwillow Books, 1985); full-color photographs; Interest Level: K-3; Reading Level: 1.5.

Contains photographs of eleven zoo animals and three words that describe each animal. The last page contains a table listing information about each animal.

***Color Zoo* by Lois Ehlert** (Philadelphia: J.B. Lippincott, 1989); full-color illustrations; Interest Level: K-3; Reading Level: 1.8.

Using clever cut-outs, the author demonstrates how shapes can be constructed to create animal faces.

***Dear Zoo* by Rod Campbell** (New York: Puffin Books, 1982); full-color illustrations; Interest Level: K-3; Reading Level: 2.0.

Lift-the-flap format contains illustrations of zoo animals.

***I Spy at the Zoo* by Maureen Roffey** (New York: Four Winds Press, 1987); full-color illustrations; Interest Level: K-3; Reading Level: 1.9.

The author introduces the reader to the familiar sights in a zoo with a game of "I Spy."

***One, Two, Number Zoo* by Gabrielle Stoddart and Martin Baker** (North Pomfret, VT: Hodder and Stoughton, 1982); full-color illustrations; Interest Level: K-3; Reading Level: 2.8.

Rhymes and illustrations about zoo animals introduce readers to numbers one to ten.

***Private Zoo* by Georgess McHargue and Michael Foreman** (New York: Viking Press, 1975); full-color illustrations; Interest Level: K-3; Reading Level: 2.5.

Unable to visit the zoo, a young boy sees the shadows of eccentric friends and family and imagines them to be animals at the zoo.

***Zoo Animals* by Michele Chopin Roosevelt** (New York: Random House, 1983); full-color illustrations; Interest Level: K-3; Reading Level: not listed.

Simple text introduces the reader to eight zoo animals.

***Zoo Song* by Barbara Bottner, illustrated by Lynn Munsinger** (New York: Scholastic, 1987); full-color illustrations; Interest Level: K-3; Reading level: 2.5.

Three zoo animals disrupt each other with their loud singing, dancing, and violin-playing until they learn to work together.

Nonfiction Resources

Eric Carle's Animals, Animals by Eric Carle (New York: Philomel Books, 1989); full-color illustrations; Interest Level: K-3; Reading Level: 3.8.

Eric Carle combines his bright, bold animal collages with an anthology of poems about each animal.

Glow-in-the-Dark Book of Animal Skeletons by Regina Kahney (New York: Random House, 1992); full-color illustrations; Interest and Reading Levels: not listed.

Using a chemical that glows in the dark, the author introduces the reader to the skeletal structure and movement of various animals including the cheetah, bat, cobra, and human.

Handtalk Zoo by George Ancona and Mary Beth Miller (New York: Four Winds Press, 1989); full-color photographs; Interest Level: 3-6; Reading Level: not listed.

Children visiting a zoo demonstrate how to say the names of the animals, as well as other common phrases, in sign language.

Syd Hoff's Animal Jokes by Syd Hoff (Philadelphia: J.B. Lippincott, 1985); full-color illustrations; Interest Level: K-3; Reading Level: 1.8.

Contains visual and verbal jokes and riddles about familiar animals.

Zoo by Gail Gibbons (New York: Thomas Y. Crowell, 1987); full-color illustrations; Interest Level: K-3; Reading Level: 4.4.

Contains a behind-the-scenes look at the management of a modern zoo and at the functions of its workers.

Recipe: Zoo Treats

1 3-3/4 oz. box instant vanilla pudding

1 20-ounce can undrained, crushed pineapple, chilled

1 17-ounce can drained fruit cocktail, chilled

1 cup shredded coconut

1 8-ounce container non-dairy whipped cream

about 9 drops of green food coloring

1 box animal crackers

This recipe makes about 12 cups. Stir the first six ingredients together in a bowl and spoon about 3/4-cup servings into individual clear plastic cups. Refrigerate one hour or more. Just before serving, place animal crackers, standing up, on the mixture.

Music Activity: "At the Zoo"

Refer to the accompanying finger plays using American Sign Language.

AT THE ZOO (Sung to the tune "The Sidewalks of New York.")

Original music by Charles Lawler and James Blake, 1894

Camel, monkey, tiger, kangaroo, lion,

alligator. All reside at City

Z o o. Zebra, bear, and e m u.

Bison, giraffe and frog.

We learn about the animals

that reside at City Z o o.

Art Activity: Zoo Pocket

Materials:

- photocopies of the lion pattern (one photocopy per child)
- 6-inch paper plates (two plates per child)
- crayons
- safety scissors
- glue
- *optional:* yarn cut into 20-inch lengths, staples, stapler

Preparation:

Cut a wedge from half of the paper plates; each child will receive a modified and unmodified paper plate.

Procedure:

Have students color and cut out the lion head and cut the radiating lines to create the mane. Glue the head to the convex side of the unmodified plate. Glue the lion's head paper plate to the paper plate with the wedge cut out, concave sides together. The wedge portion should be at the top. For greater strength, staple along the rim. (For greater versatility, staple a 20-inch length of yarn onto either side of the rim to create a necklace effect.) When the glue is dried, the pocket may be used to carry lightweight items.

Lion Pattern

Name _____ Date _____

Classroom Teacher _____

Zoo Research Project: Animals are amazing. Use an almanac or book of world records to look up "animal." Answer the questions below:

1. Which animal is the largest? _____

2. Which animal is the noisiest? _____

3. Which animal is the fastest? _____

4. Which animal is the most poisonous? _____

5. Which animal is the strongest? _____

Write the title of the book where you found your information.

_____

_____

Celebrate Zoo Month in June.

Appendix

Creative Classroom Learning Extensions
for Letters A to Z

A: Use the list of endangered species to create an endangered species mural. Ask the local newspaper to photograph it.

B: Use common objects to create bubble wands. Test them to see if they work.

C: Read about Smokey the Bear. Use that information to create fire prevention posters. Donate the posters to national, state, local, and/or private parks.

D: Create a dinosaur dictionary. Send it to a paleontologist at a natural history museum for his/her opinion.

E: Decorate eggs with everyday objects to create an "eggs-citing" fashion show and display. Invite other classrooms to view the display.

F: Designate one day as Frog Day. Write poems, draw pictures, wear green, and determine other ways to celebrate those lovable green critters.

G: Collect and collate gingerbread recipes to create a gingerbread cookbook for each student.

H: Visit an animal shelter. Create posters to help find homes for the animals. Display the posters around town.

I: Create insects with different objects and display in the classroom.

J: Choose a commercial company that produces jam and jelly from stock market listings. Purchase one share of the stock. Monitor the progress of the stock each day. Decide how to use the profit, if there is any, at the end of the year.

K: Have the classroom brainstorm proclamations they would issue if they were rulers of the world. Collect the ideas into a booklet to give as gifts to parents.

L: Have students create stories, poems, and pictures about love. Place the creations on the Internet.

M: Visit a gila monster at a local pet store. Ask the pet store manager how to care for gila monsters and other exotic pets.

N: Tape record the class as it sings one or two lullabies. Place the recording on an electronic answering service and connect it to a school telephone during nonbusiness hours. Encourage students and their younger siblings to call the service for a lullaby just before they go to bed.

O: Use the concept of proportion to create cardboard planets drawn to scale. Hang the planets in the school in relative distance to each other.

P: Have students bring in coins from other countries. Compare and contrast the coins with U.S. coins. Send students to other classrooms to show and explain the coin connection.

Q: Give each child graph paper, colored pencils and a ruler, and have them create a geometric quilt. Ask a local fabric store to display the creations.

R: Visit a local grocery store to view the many products that grow in countries that have large tropical rain forests. Those products include: bananas, rice, sugar, corn, cotton, soybeans, fruits, cassava, coca, tobacco, hemp, coconuts, rubber, ginger, molasses, sweet potatoes, palm products, beans, fish, pepper, and medicine. Explore the possibility of the school cafeteria serving some of the foods for a tropical rain forest meal.

S: Write a letter of introduction and send it to an English teacher in Italy. Ask for a response to the letter from his or her students. Perhaps the students can become pen pals.

T: Using the turtle's example of moving forward at a slow and steady pace, have the class set a long-term goal. Consistently take time each day to work on achieving the goal. Plan a celebration when the goal is reached.

U: Send a message in a bottle to another class inviting them to participate in an undersea treasure hunt. Devise clues and riddles throughout the school and playground to lead the class to the treasure.

V: Invite a travel agent to visit the classroom and discuss his or her job. Ask the agent to bring travel brochures to share with the students.

W: Using an electronic answering machine hooked up to a school telephone during nonbusiness hours, create a daily weather forecast. Have each child, in turn, read and record the forecast.

X: Think of an extra-special project to benefit the elderly, such as afternoon teas with book or poetry readings.

Y: Have students lie on a large piece of paper and draw each other's outline. Cut out the outline and color. Hang them up for display. Have students take turns writing complimentary words on each outline about the child.

Z: Create a money-making project (e.g., book fair, bake sale, flea market) to adopt an animal at a local zoo or to provide a donation for endangered species.